PACKARD
THE PRIDE

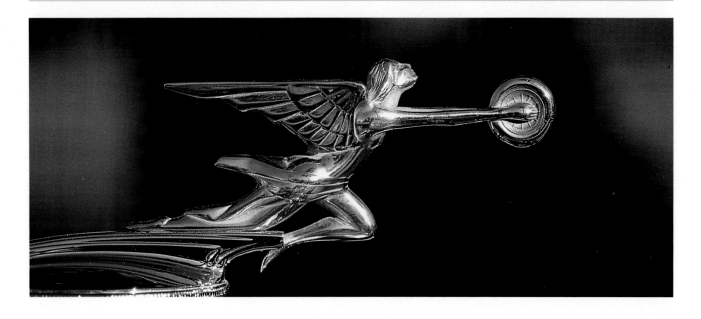

PACKARD
THE PRIDE

BY J. M. FENSTER

PHOTOGRAPHY BY ROY D. QUERY

DESIGN BY MICHAEL PARDO

AUTOMOBILE QUARTERLY PUBLICATIONS

AUTOMOBILE QUARTERLY PUBLICATIONS

Editor & Publisher
GERRY DURNELL

Associate Publisher
KAYE BOWLES-DURNELL

Chief Operations Officer, Technical Editor
JOHN C. DURNELL

Managing Editor
TRACY POWELL

Art & Design
ALFRED MORESCHI

Founding Editor & Publisher
L. SCOTT BAILEY

Editor for this book: Montgomery Frayne

Automobile Quarterly Publications
Automobile Heritage Publishing and Communications, LLC.

Library of Congress Catalog Number: 89-84046
ISBN 0-9711468-2-9 (previously ISBN 0-915038-66-8)
Automobile Quarterly Publications

CONTENTS

INTRODUCTION

I
N 1937, PACKARD set up a Customer Relations department in order to answer letters and fulfill special requests.

A man from Texas wrote to ask if Packard could help get his daughter committed to a mental institution. It couldn't, or if it could, it didn't. Later, the office received a letter from a man digging ditches for a living, who wrote that he considered the owning of a Packard to be the "acme of human achievement." Far from trying to have him committed to a Texas mental institution, the head of the department devoted two days to composing a response with the proper degree of respect and encouragement. Three years later, the ditch-digger wrote again—this time, he said, as the owner of a Packard car.

In its day, Packard was the flagship American car the way that Rolls-Royce still fills that role in England. No one would accuse a person of un-American activities for buying a Pierce Arrow or a Duesenberg, but Packard was built into the system as a symbol of success that everyone recognized.

The wife of a vice president at Hupmobile had no compunction about telling her husband to buy her a new Packard in 1930. Henry Ford went to his grave in a Packard. Enzo Ferrari was first inspired to think in terms of 12-cylinder engines by the sound of the Packard Twin Six cars driven by American Army officers in World War I. "The harmonious voice of this engine," he called it. And Ettore Bugatti, showing his gracious side, was known to despise Packards less than he despised other non-Bugattis.

Next to Ford, *Fortune* magazine considered Packard the most valuable name in the auto industry in 1937: "For a

generation its luxurious cars had never carried lesser folk than rich invalids to their airings, diplomats to embassies, gangsters to funerals, stars to the studios, war lords through Chinese dust, heroes through ticker tape, heiresses across Long Island and Grosse Pointe."

The company liked to refer to "1000 distinguished families

who had owned Packard cars for more than 21 years"—a club of sorts. W.F.R. Murrie, head of the Hershey Chocolate Company, bought 45 new Packards in 35 years: He was in the club. He even had one of his Packards painted to match the color of a chocolate bar. In advertising, the company mentioned the names of the distinguished 1000, but did not show their faces, depicting instead the gates to their driveways.

When a Packard ad did show a face, it was an idealized face. In November 1926, *Country Life* was a magazine so assured that its real estate ads could promote tracts that were "socially selective" or "highly restricted." Rolls-Royce's ad in that issue showed a woodblock print of a horsewoman. Packard's ad showed a town car next to an oil painting. The painting was of two couples sitting in a box at a concert, and it must have been the most excruciatingly boring evening any of them had ever endured. "The Restful Car," the ad promised; the four of them are clearly thinking of precisely that and the ride home.

In December, Chrysler's ad was a stylish and colorful illustration of a woman driving up to a canopied apartment building. Either she's home or—more fun—she's not home. Packard's advertisement for the next issue showed a limousine with a painting of ''Beauty,'' a woman in green, standing next to an urn, holding a green feather fan, eyes dully glazed (apparently wondering why she couldn't have been picked for the Chrysler ad). For February, Packard depicted ''Prestige,'' which was a sedan next to a painting of a dinner party. An ambassador of some sort has been seated next to a woman wearing a tiara. Anyone would feel sorry for them. Resigned though they seem, it is transparent that they would even rather be at that concert.

Such was the life of the ideal Packard customer—so distinguished, so noble, so socially selective, and so stoic throughout. Of course, the real-life Packard customers fit no such description: They laughed probably, and blinked almost definitely. At the core of the real-life customer, however, was the aspiration to such eminent, exquisite ennui. Therein lies respectability—and therein lies the commodity that Packard put on wheels: fine, American respectability. Chocolate-company presidents knew it, women in tiaras knew it, and best of all, ditch-diggers knew it.

Even the gang at the Hupmobile Company Christmas party knew it.

This book is an informal study of the real-life Packard owners and others, especially coachbuilders, who surrounded individual cars. As has been noted, the Packard company made a thorough record of its own impression of its customers—or some calculated version of them. Those customers had, however, more than names and gates.

Louise Boyd of San Rafael, California, was commissioned by the American Geographic Society to write a book on a trip through rural Poland in 1935. Just before she left, she bought a Packard Twelve convertible sedan by Dietrich. Someone reading this, in her subsequent book, *Polish Countrysides*, might assume that she had picked out nice luggage for the trip and then had the car built to match. However, Miss Boyd was a serious explorer, the veteran of a half-dozen Arctic expeditions, and she conquered mishap with meticulous preparation. If she bought a new Packard for the trip, it was because she thought it wouldn't break down or get stuck or make her road-weary, and hers did not. That it should also be one of the most stunning cars ever seen in or out of rural Poland is the sort of fortuitous circumstance that people like Miss Boyd find easy to effect.

A.G. Stoltz of Bucyrus, Ohio, was far ahead of his time in the car-collector hobby, which was not just a hobby but more

of an eccentricity, when he bought his Custom Super Clipper in 1947. As a banker, he bought the car to preserve it, certain that it was a future classic. This was long before F40 Ferraris and 959 Porsches were being snapped up like high-tech Hummels, instant collectibles. Stoltz believed that nobody built a car as well as Packard in 1947 and that not even Packard could sustain its level of quality in the market that was developing. Though he sold the Packard in 1960, he has been proven right about the status of his car.

William Hunter, another banker, adored his 1905 Model N Packard, and that was notable because he was one of Philadelphia's most enthusiastic horsemen. Hunter never sold his Packard—a distinct sign of character—but after his death in 1932, it was purchased by Hyde Ballard, who appreciated it in kind.

In 1940, Ballard wrote about driving vintage Packards for the *Bulletin* of the Antique Automobile Club of America: ''Not infrequently I see a face light up with a familiar gleam. 'We had the first one like it that came to town,' or 'Look! An old second series just like the one we took to the top of Pike's Peak,' or 'Our car was just like that, and the only one to get through the flood of 1918!' ''

On paper, the Packard Motor Car Company belonged to its 107,000 shareholders. Its vast record of accomplishment is the legacy of Messrs. Packard, Schmidt, Joy, Macauley, Vincent, and the others who worked at Packard. But pride in the Packard automobile belonged to Boyd, Stoltz, Hunter . . . and anybody who survived the Arctic Circle or the ''flood of 1918.'' If I were asked who it was that made Packard great, I would start naming just those names, and the list would hardly end at 1000.

—*Julie M. Fenster*

ACKNOWLEDGEMENTS

When Tom Fetch drove a one-cylinder Packard across the country in 1903, he actually learned to avoid the good roads he found, because they usually led to farmhouses. Those, however, are exactly the roads taken in the journey that this book represents.

Only two of the Packards in this volume were owned by famous people, those being George Patton, who owned the 1932 seven-passenger sedan, and Jean Harlow, who owned the 1932 sport phaeton. The other owners led unassuming lives. Why are they being profiled?

Because they once owned a Packard car.

Anybody who studies Packards relies on the book *PACKARD: A History of the Motor Car and the Company* (Princeton, New Jersey: Princeton Publishing, 1978), edited by Beverly Rae Kimes. Another general resource was *Saga of Packard* by Fred Adams (Detroit: Packard Motor Car Company, 1949).

Over 280 newspaper articles were consulted, predominantly from *The New York Times* and *The Evening-Bulletin* (Philadelphia). Walter Miller kindly made available his automotive literature inventory.

The selection of the cars was based on these factors: model, style, condition, color, history, and location. Some stand out in certain categories: The goal was a balance throughout the book. The following historians made valuable suggestions: Bill Snyder, Howard Schavitz, Don Weber, Brad Skinner, Bob Turnquist, Neal Donovan, Robert Escalante, James Pearsall, Jim Brodes, Jim Tuschinsky, Robert Erausquin, Stuart and Stella Blond, Neil Torrence, and the staffs of Packards International and the Eastern Packard Club. Randy Ema made contributions to the book at every turn.

James Ward Packard donated the first Packard—and $1 million for a Mechanical and Electrical Engineering Building—to Lehigh University. The board of Packard, conducting itself with decorum befitting an automaker (or a foreign ministry), thereupon issued a Resolution citing J.W. for "insuring to that institution a greatly augmented equipment." Barbara A. Dolan, college relations officer, arranged for photography; Dr. Tom Jackson, professor emeritus, has cared for the car since the Thirties. Terry Martin lent his expertise on Warren, Ohio, and Warren-Packards. Photo credit: Jim Brodes.

John Jones restored the 1905 Model N for its previous owner, and when the opportunity came along to buy it, he did not hesitate. Alan Ballard supplied background material, as did the Free Library of Philadelphia and the Photojournalism Collection at Temple University. Hunter's monograph, "Devon and Its Historic Surroundings," and other documents were provided by the Chester County (Pennsylvania) Historical Society; the quotes from *The Automobile* appeared November 5, 1904. Photo credit: John and Carol Jones.

Marshall Mathews caught his friend Phil Hill at a weak moment and managed to buy the 1912 brougham from him. Brad Skinner supplied details about the history of the car. The quote on Kansas City is from *Abroad At Home* by Julian Street (New York: The Century Co. 1914). Color photography site: San Jose Historical Museum turn-of-the-century town. Photo credit: Marshall and Nancy Mathews.

The 1913 phaeton runabout has been in the collection of Robert and Lillian Robinson for about 15 years. I am grateful to Don Weber, an authority on the Packard Six. Photo credit: AQ Archives.

"We wish he'd never sold it," Sherman Comings said of his father and the 1917 Twin Six phaeton, now owned by Marshall Mathews. Sherman and Richard Comings enthusiastically recalled the car and their family for this book. Further cooperation came from Mathews, Philip Hatton, Bill Barker, the Bancroft Library of the University of California at Berkeley, the California State Library, and the Monterey Library. Photo credit: Mr. and Mrs. Sherman Comings.

John King bought the 1920 Twin Six roadster by Rubay as a disassembled jumble in 1964, from a collector in Tulsa, Oklahoma. The restoration was finally completed in 1984. Concerning the life and work of Léon Rubay, the following were valuable sources: the Western Reserve Historical Society in Cleveland; Henry Merkel; *Golden Wheels: The Story of the Automobiles Made in Cleveland and Northeastern Ohio, 1892-1932* by Richard Wager (Cleveland: The Western Reserve Historical Society and the Cleveland Automobile Club, 1975); "Léon Rubay—Coachmaker" by Edward J. Blend Jr.

(*Antique Automobile*: May 1965); and Rubay Carrosserie Automobile booklets, c. 1920. The quote regarding Paris is from *The Days Before Yesterday* by Lord Frederic Hamilton (London: Hodder and Stoughton, 1920). Photo credit: The Western Reserve Historical Society.

Howard Henry still has the 1924 Pennsylvania title for his 1925 touring car, and it pleases him to think that the next owner will be his nephew, the grandson of the first owner. Ernest Perks, at 92, graciously recalled his years as chauffeur. The opening quote is from *Plant Life 1950* edited by H.P. Traub and H.N. Moldenke (Stanford: The American Plant Life Society, 1950); another source was "Seeing America First—Nonstop" by George Hamlin (*The Cormorant*: Spring 1973). Photo credit: Howard G. Henry.

L. Morgan Yost made a fundamental contribution to *PACKARD: A History of the Motor Car and the Company*, writing about Packard between the wars. This book features his 1926 convertible coupe by Dietrich. I am grateful to the Sterling (Illinois) Library, John Ridge Jr., and John Ridge III. Photo credit: National Automotive History Collection (N.A.H.C.) of the Detroit Public Library.

The Vassar sophomore of the opening story in the chapter on the 1926 landaulet by LeBaron was none other than the mother of Mrs. Judith Ogden Henry, whose husband owns the car today. At 95, Mary B. Ogden remembers Glenn Stewart, and to corroborate, Mrs. Henry telephoned the roommate mentioned in the story, Miss Glenn Means. Adolph Pretzler, the Stewarts' former driver and estate manager, could not have been kinder. Other sources were the Yale University Alumni Records Office; *The Geographical Review* (Spring 1932); *Wye Island* by Boyd Gibbons (Baltimore: Johns Hopkins University, 1977); letter from Hugo Pfau to H.G. Henry, 1973. Photo credit: Adolph Pretzler.

Phil Hill has a collection of 11 Packards. Any of them would be an asset to a book like this one. I am sincerely grateful to Strother MacMinn, Jude Long of the Morro Bay Library, and Mary Moses and Glenn Kleinhammer, both of Morro Bay. Photo credit: Phil Hill.

Dr. Joseph Hossbacher purchased the 1928 standard sedan from Mrs. Geronimo and her son, Wilbur, in 1962. Photo credit: N.A.H.C.

The 1929 626 speedster is on display at the Henry Ford Museum & Greenfield Village, in Dearborn, Michigan. Thanks to the following people, though, it had a day off for the photography in this book: Steven Hamp, Randy Mason, and Nancy Diem. Montgomery Young, the previous owner, lent information about the car and lent, too, great doses of encouragement. Photo credit: Monty Young.

Larry Waterhouse is an executive at Ford, but his first loyalty may be to Waterhouse and Co., since he is the grandson of one of the founders. He supplied material regarding Waterhouse. I am indebted, too, to Mark Smith, who owns the car, Dr. D.F. Shields, and George Jepson. The quote is from ''The Waterhouse Story'' by S.J. Dunham (*The Classic Car*: September 1969). Color photography site: Pebble Beach, California. Photo credit: Larry Waterhouse.

Mr. and Mrs. Frank Miller have liked Packards all their lives, since both of them grew up in Packard families, in California. The sources regarding the career of Maurice Proux, who built their 1930 Packard, were issues of *l'equipement automobile* and *Auto-Carrosserie, 1928-1933*. Photo credit: Mr. and Mrs. Frank Miller.

The third owners of Jean Harlow's 1932 sport phaeton used it to tow their trailer. In 1964, they sold it to Cliff and Joyce Gooding, who treasure the car. Brian Bundy, an expert on Harlow, was very helpful. Photo credit: Cliff and Joyce Gooding.

The salesman who bought George Patton's 1932 seven-passenger sedan from the general's family drove it 255,000 miles. When Fred and Carol Mauck discovered it, it was in a dirt-floor garage, up to its hubcaps in dirt floor. Fred restored everything himself, except for the engine. I am sincerely grateful to the Patton family and Ruth Patton Totten in particular. Further material on Patton is from *The Patton Papers* (Boston: Houghton Mifflin, 1976). Photo credit: 3rd Cavalry Museum, Fort Bliss, Texas.

Jerry Bell bought a dilapidated Light Eight in 1962. He paid $700 and was told that it had belonged to the Stetson family. Bell restored the car himself and liked to tell inquirers that it was a new Cadillac. I am thankful to Thurman and Dee Decker, Jerry Bell Jr., Jeffrey Hammers, and Temple University. Photo credit: Auto-foto.

Some of the text in the chapter on the 1933-34 Car of the Dome originally appeared in *Automobile Quarterly*, Volume 25, Number 1. I am grateful now as then to Otis Chandler. The quote is from *A Century of Progress* (Chicago: 1934). Photo credit: Otis Chandler.

Bill Hirsch bought his first Packard when he was 14 years old, raising the money by cashing in his war bonds. In tracing Louise Boyd's story, I am thankful to the Marin County (California) Historical Society. The quote is from *Polish Countrysides* by Louise Boyd (New York: American Geographical Society, 1937). Other sources were *The New York Times* (September 17, 1972) and *Marin County Historical Society Magazine* (volume XIV, number 2). Photo credit: American Geographical Society.

An ambition of this book was to set certain cars against related ones in the background. Bob Bahre's collection accommodated this plan. In tracing the life of the late Frederick Hussey, original owner of the 1934 sport phaeton, the assistance of his son, Derrick, was invaluable. I am also indebted to Skip Lawrence at the Alumni Office of Haverford College, the Sussex County Historical Society, Bob Turnquist, and Chris Carlton. Photo credit: Derrick Hussey.

Wallace Walmsley supplied most of his own story about the 1937 115-C. Photo credit: The San Diego Historical Society.

In the research for the chapter on the 1937 coupe, thanks are due to Mrs. Gloria Malumphy, John Peterson, Paul Driscoll, and Mark McEachern. Photography site: Gaylordsville Garage, Gaylordsville, Connecticut. Photo credit: The Torrington Historical Society.

When Robert Meyer was growing up, his father had a 1931 convertible coupe by LeBaron, ''Ole Packard,'' that was used as a tow truck on the family farm in California. After a complete restoration, the former tow truck earned a first in class at Pebble Beach. In researching the 1938 phaeton, I am grateful to Rudy Creteur and the Princeton University Library. Sources for quotes were *The Iraq Times* (April 5, 1939); *The New York Times* (March 6, 1937); *The Classic Car* (Summer, Fall 1960); and *Uneasy Lies the Head* by King Hussein (New York: B. Geis and Assoc., 1962). Photo credit: AQ archives.

Ken Gibson bought the 1940 station sedan ''woodie'' because he collects vintage ''woodie'' boats. I am indebted to Bruce A. Kresge M.D., the K Mart Corp., Bud Shaw, Frank Buck, and the Kresge Foundation. Quotes were from *S.S. Kresge* by Stanley S. Kresge (Pennsylvania: Newcomen, 1957); *The New York Times* (October 19, 1966). Photo Credit: Nina Leen, Life Magazine C Time Inc.

During the summer of 1940, Gene Tareshawty got a ride in a maroon Darrin victoria with a tan interior. Twenty-eight years later, he bought a Darrin and refurbished it in maroon and tan. Today, he owns seven Darrin-Packards. The previous owner of the 1940 sport sedan, J. David Lee, supplied much valuable material; Tom Mix was helpful, too. Photo credit: J. David Lee Collection.

In the research on Jerry Peterson's 1941 formal sedan, Mr. and Mrs. Peterson, George Pillsbury, and the Minnesota Historical Society all helped. Photo credit: Mr. and Mrs. George Pillsbury.

The 1941 convertible victoria is displayed in Victoria, British Columbia. Photo credit: The Classic Car Museum, owned by Murray Gammon. Alistair Frame and Alan Reid were very helpful, as were Don Williams and Chris Bohman. Photo credit: Randy Ema.

Rick and Sue Reale not only love their 1941 Clipper, they love their son, too, and named him John Packard Reale. I am grateful to these residents of Meriden: Mr. and Mrs. Frank Mellon, Larry Miller, and Kay Cooke. Photo credit: Mr. and Mrs. Frank Mellon.

I was told of a super Custom Super Clipper, but no one knew its whereabouts. I am grateful to Stuart Bewley, the present owner, for responding to inquiries. I am indebted, too, to Neil Torrence, The Auction, and Nick Stoltz. Photo credit: Nick Stoltz.

In telling the story of the 1952 Mayfair convertible, I am especially grateful to Murray Gammon, as it is his story, too; another set of thanks to Messrs. Frame and Reid. Photo credit: Murray Gammon.

Bob McAtee was president of Packards International from 1983-87; of the 19 Packards he has owned over the years, the 1954 Patrician is his favorite. Photo credit: N.A.H.C.

Dick Teague's 1956 Caribbean hardtop is just part of his Packard collection. Photo credit: Dick Teague. It has been a while since a hot scoop came out of the Packard Motor Car Company, but Mr. Teague's 1999 Packard is news. Ken Eberts made the rendering.

In the introduction to The Early Years, the tire gauge is from the collection of Fred and Carol Mauck. In the introduction to The Classic Years, the cartoon is from a booklet published by Earl C. Anthony in 1928, for the Los Angeles Auto Show; It is from the collection of Walter Miller. Sources were *Life's Picture History of Western Man* (New York: Time, Inc., 1951); *My Years With General Motors* by Alfred Sloan Jr. (Garden City: Doubleday, 1964); *The Nation* (June 12, 1929); *American Automobile Workers 1900-33* by J.S. Peterson (Albany: State University of New York, 1987). The original neon in the introduction to The Final Years is owned by Gene Tareshawty.

This book is dedicated to my family and to Sunny. —JMF

Early Years
1899-1920

COLOR PHOTOGRAPHY was first used successfully in 1848, when a softly pretty picture was made of a rose and amber street in Paris. The process was based on potato starch. After that, color pictures were not made very much until just about 1939—when Dorothy Gale opened her front door on Munchkinland in *The Wizard of Oz*. In the ensuing 100 years, the daily life of the world might as well have been conducted in black, white, and sepia: women in white shirtwaists sitting on the lawn; men in black bowlers standing at the curb; rows of gray shrubbery pictured in the garden magazines; the charcoal Pacific in *National Geographic*.

The colors, though, were there. Millicent Fenwick, the former congresswoman and ambassador, grew up in Bernardsville, New Jersey, the daughter of Ogden Hammond, ambassador to Spain from 1926-29. The Hammonds owned a 1912 Packard Eighteen runabout. "I remember it so well," Mrs. Fenwick said. "Two tufted black leather armchairs, yellow backs, with a monogram. Also a little yellow stool on the back. I remember my parents going for a spin on a weekend afternoon. Daddy wore goggles, and a cap with a visor, and clips on his trouser cuffs. The Packard was tricky—once he broke his arm when he started it up. Mother wore a big hat, covered by a veil with a plastic patch to look through—a veil that came down into her white linen coat with big pearl buttons. White gloves came last. Cars were for sport—horses for church and the train."

Cars were for sport, and early Packards slipped easily into

the hands of people known as good "whips." Whips handled carriages and sleighs in the winter. They were hearty, well-off, and attracted to Packard cars: "handsome models not in any sense a mere copy of other existing vehicles," in the words of a 1901 edition of *Scientific American*.

Autos crawled all over the globe in the hands of adven-

turous whips. Mrs. Fisher took a Locomobile around the world; E.R. Thomas drove one of his namesake cars through Serbia and Bulgaria; a couple of Harvard boys took a Benz across Canada; Mr. and Mrs. Glidden nipped into the Arctic Circle with a Napier.

"No small boy is so completely absorbed in his Christmas train of cars as is the contemporary public with this toy," said *Scribner's* magazine in 1907. The toy was the automobile, of course, but it could have been the countryside itself: the landscape and the horizon, a toy indeed in the eyes of a weary industrial world enjoying a second childhood. The machine in the family garage could lead to anywhere, anytime. To anywhere.

As much as any make, Packard seemed to agitate the mad mobility of the new century. In 1903, a company employee named Tom Fetch drove a Model F Packard, called "Old Pacific," coast-to-coast in 61 days. "The deserts of Utah and the mountains of Colorado were not as bad as the mud of

Iowa," Fetch told *The New York Times*. Company employees took a Packard Thirty to Cuba in 1908, and the same year, the factory supported one man's family on a cross-country trip in a Packard.

The inclination of a company to reap publicity from an automobile-adventure is plain. However, private citizens were even more motivated. Melvin Hall, a 21-year-old Vermonter, drove his mother around the world in a Packard Six in 1911-13, and for good measure, they drove even farther into the Arctic Circle than had the Gliddens.

L.L. Whitman drove a Packard 1100 miles through California in 1908, replacing the tonneau top with a doorman's umbrella. Mrs. Caroline Thurber took one to Norway the next year. After 23 hours of constant driving, her party reached a valley called Rohdal, where an innkeeper assured them that they couldn't possibly have crossed the mountains. "You couldn't have found the road," he said. "And certainly, you couldn't have crossed the pass. No motor has ever done it. The road is quite impossible for your machine and besides, *it is forbidden.*"

"But we did," Mrs. Thurber replied, with precocious satisfaction.

Being the first to do or see something has enthralled Americans and Europeans since Christopher Columbus. "The road grew dim and gloomy, although it was midday," L.L. Whitman wrote of the trip to Yosemite in his parasol-Packard. "The warden of the Lodge there said we were the first automobilists to come to the place."

The last frontier was supposed to have been closed by 1890. It is to be remembered, though, that the first person to take the mountain pass to Rohdal, Norway, was Caroline Thurber and that the first automobile in a certain part of Yosemite was that of L.L. Whitman.

James Ward Packard and his brother, William Doud Packard, owned an electric parts company in Warren, Ohio, when they became automobilists in 1898. That is the year that James Packard bought a Winton.

James took many trips to test his one-cylinder model, once to Buffalo and often to his home near Chautauqua. If he had had his way, the company would have stayed with the one-cylinder car, the trouble-free one-cylinder. He even published a booklet against multiple cylinders, called "Six to One, or Wasted Pride, Perspiration, and Profanity." It failed to turn the tide, though, and in 1902, Packard made a two-cylinder, and then, in 1903, a four-cylinder car.

By then, a force by the name of Henry B. Joy had taken over. If James had been timid at the wheel of the new company, Henry Joy stepped on the gas.

First, Joy made the Packard Motor Car Company a fashionable investment for old Detroit fortunes, one of which was his. Next, he had the operation moved to Detroit. For James Packard, though, Warren remained the center of the universe. Without abandoning the car company, he turned back to the electric parts business (later sold to General Motors). He became an important watch collector in his old age, spending $16,000 in 1922 for a Patek Philippe watch: It showed the moon phases as they appeared from his bedroom window in Warren, the center of the universe.

Henry Joy started out with a first-rate engineering staff in Detroit, to which he added a genius named Jesse Vincent as chief engineer in 1912. Vincent's single greatest accomplishment was the Twin Six engine, introduced in 1915. He would stay with the company until 1954, hiring, in turn, superb engineers throughout the ranks.

By 1915, Joy was already assuming that the United States would enter World War I. As a patriotic gesture, and because of his personal interest in aviation, he directed Packard engineers to devote their time to the development of an airplane engine. The result was the Liberty engine (largely the work of Vincent), and it was ready when the country did enter the War on April 6, 1917—and, more importantly, on July 14 when the Congress appropriated $640 million for a military aviation program.

By World War I, the car was being put to all of the uses only predicted for it much earlier. In 1901, Vickers of England paraded a "war car" through the streets—a tank in all but name. In 1902, H.C. Frick, the steel magnate, started using a car to commute the 14 miles to his office in Pittsburgh, and he calculated that the time he saved was worth $500,000 per year to him. At the start, though, cars were for sport.

William Hunter of Devon, Pennsylvania, revered his 1905 Packard Model N, a car that is featured in the following pages. Some Friday or Saturday nights after he went to sleep, his sons William and Edmond would steal the huge car out of the garage. They'd put the top down and ease it out of the driveway, north onto Waterloo Road, slowing when they reached the triple tracks of the Pennsylvania Railroad Main Line. The only light came from the blond glow of the acetylene lamps on their own car and perhaps from the stars or the moon. Waterloo Road ended at Lancaster Pike, and on the Pike, they set the Packard loose, plowing into the silence of the night at 75 mph. Black was the air, and white was the whizzing streak of the lights: black and white.

1899 Model A Single-Seat Roadster

ONE MILLION six hundred and ten thousand Packard cars began in July 1899, with one: a single-cylinder Model A. All of the others were built for profit, but the first was never even for sale. The company it spawned kept it, at first for reference, then for publicity, and then like something inherited from a distant relative, something wondrous but practically useless.

In 1930, the progenitor of all Packards was donated to Lehigh University, alma mater of James Ward Packard. Lehigh treats the little relic like a national treasure; it is on display in the lobby of the Packard Laboratory of Mechanical and Electrical Engineering, biding the years in a glass case. At Lehigh, they call it "A-1."

Every three years or so, a special occasion persuades the University to bring A-1 out into the open air. In 1974, it was returned to its birthplace, Warren, Ohio, to lead a parade commemorating the 75th anniversary of the founding of the Packard Motor Car Company. With a top speed of 20 mph, it ran faithfully through the streets, from the site on which it was built to Courthouse Square, where Warren residents lined up just to get a good look at an 1899 Packard car.

Residents of Warren must have been just as curious in the autumn of 1899, not about something old, but about something very, very new: an 1899 Packard car.

The Model A rolled out of the factory on the afternoon of November 6, 1899, with James Packard at the controls. The first Packard was carefully constructed, "superior to any on

The first Packard had a long career as a curio, here at a 1933 exhibition in New York.

the market" in the opinion of the worldly wise *Warren Daily Chronicle*, though early photographs of the chassis betray a sloppy blotch of solder, in the shape of West Virginia, on the water tank.

The prototype car has two forward gears and one reverse; the single-cylinder engine is water-cooled and transmits

power to the rear wheels through a chain drive. A brake drum is mounted alongside the chain's sprocket on the rear axle. The body was ordered from a Warren carriage-builder, in wood with leather mudguards, dashboard, and upholstery.

To start the car on November 6, 1899, James Packard or some husky apprentice had to crank the high-compression engine, applying an even higher-compression shoulder to the task. Mr. Packard then climbed up to the seat and used the transmission levers to engage the gearing; soon after, a single stick replaced the levers, employing an "H" pattern: Reverse is to the left and forward; low, to the left and back; high, to the right and back, and the transmission brake, to the right and forward. In Packard's version of the planetary transmission, no clutch was necessary.

The car chugs at low speeds but runs smoothly with momentum. In 1899, so many dogs chased it, Mr. Packard had to buy the first Packard accessory: an ammonia squirt gun.

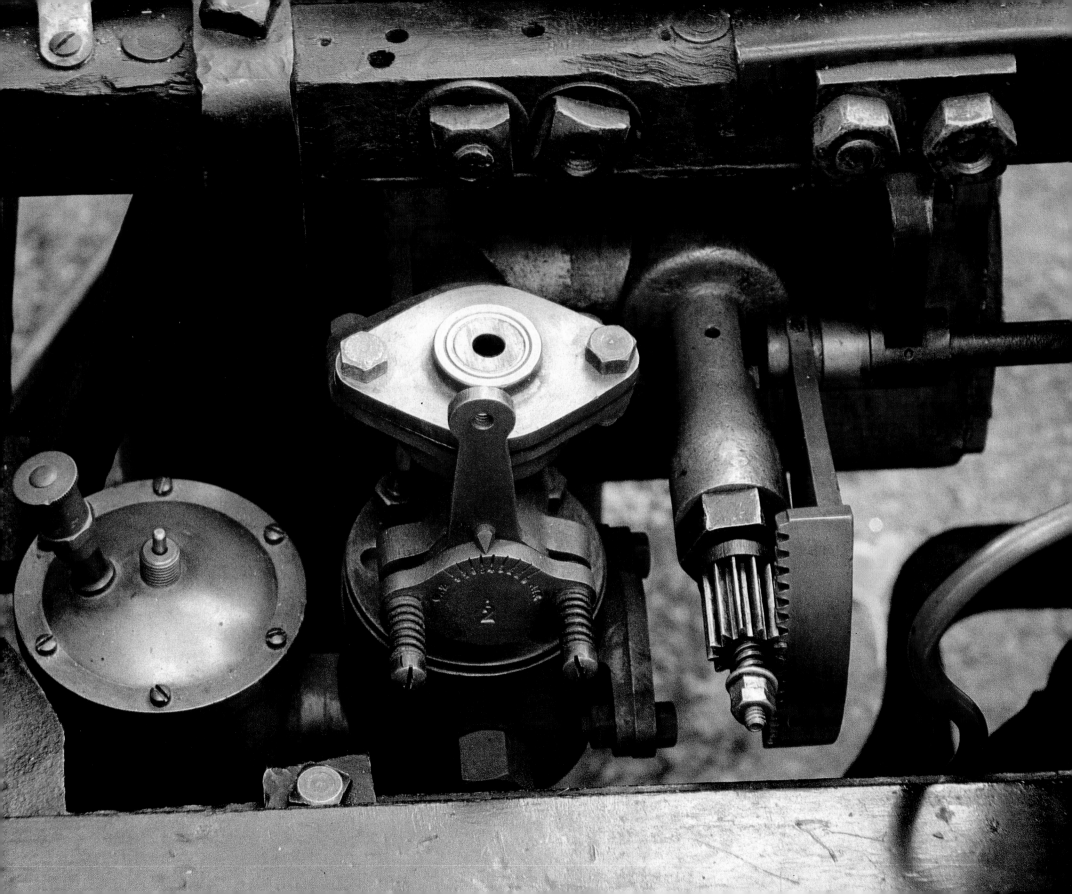

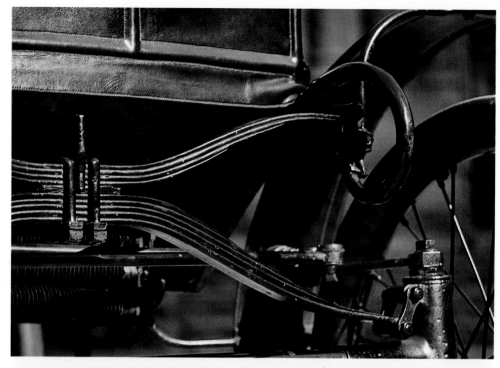

When Lehigh brought A-1 to Ohio in 1974, Packard historian Terry Martin surrendered to suspicious thoughts: What if the Lehigh car was a fraud—a reproduction, or Packard car number three, four, or five . . . ? During the celebration, Martin spirited the car off to a back room, beknownst to no one, and pulled the rear deck off.

The first Packard was not tagged with a serial or engine number—at the time, there was no number two with which to confuse it. It has something better than a number, though: a blotch of solder in the shape of West Virginia. Martin located it at once and was assured; numbers lie, but solder, as a rule, does not.

It was a fantastic car, the first Packard, a rough draft, a dress rehearsal, a dry run that could have been anything at all, but what it was, was a success. Had it not been, the Packard brothers might not have decided to build six more.

1905 Model N Touring Car

NINETEEN-OH-FIVE and the world held no surprises for the Packard Motor Car Company. At six years old, it had its home on East Grand Boulevard in Detroit; it had its stake in the business of automobiles; and it had a reputation that commanded respect in the carnival of early auto youngbloods. The Model N, the company's only product for 1905, was absolutely enormous for its day, yet "distinctly 'Packard' throughout," to *The Automobile*, showing "many marks of simplicity and directness of action of all the parts."

The Model N was the company's ninth model, a direct successor to the sturdy Model L of 1904. The L had been a keen success for Packard, with sales of 207, but the N nearly doubled that figure, employing a slightly larger version of the same four-cylinder engine, this one cast in France, and a chassis that was longer by a foot.

A stock Model L Packard had caused a great buzz in August 1904, by covering 1000 nonstop miles at an average speed of 33.5 mph. Without attempting any records, Packard promised that the Model N would easily maintain 45 mph on country roads. The landscape being largely unpaved in '05, those roads would be smoothed by the car's well-tested transverse front springing, which placed the weight of the car at the wheels and thereby reduced twisting.

To fascinate the driver with the N's ability to scale steep hills, hills that would smother lesser cars, the dashboard was fitted with a Yankee Grade Meter, which measured the steep-

In 1922, William Hunter's '05 Model N was already on display as an antique.

ness of an incline as a percentage.

In its preview, *The Automobile* called the Model N "a lightweight, flexible, active touring car of 23-28 horsepower, designed to meet in every respect the requirements of the modern user, be he an enthusiastic tourist or only one in need of the perfect family car."

William T. Hunter was both. He bought a Model N touring car in 1905 and still owned it when he died in 1933. In 1936, it was purchased by Hyde Ballard, an early member of the Antique Automobile Club of America; at that club's very first outing on June 18, 1938, the touring car was still fresh, earning first prize in the Engine Starting Contest.

William Hunter was a sportsman, and in 1910, he revived the Devon (Pennsylvania) Horse Show, still an event of national importance. He had sharp features, lively blue eyes, and a robust mustache worthy of Theodore Roosevelt. A banker and private investor, he divided his time between New York and Philadelphia, with three months each year in Europe.

At the age of 45 in 1905, Hunter lived with his wife and three children in Devon, on Philadelphia's Main Line. Hunter's own view of Devon reveals his imagination: "Every road," he wrote, "passes over historic ground, every path has its legend, each old house its traditions." He was an

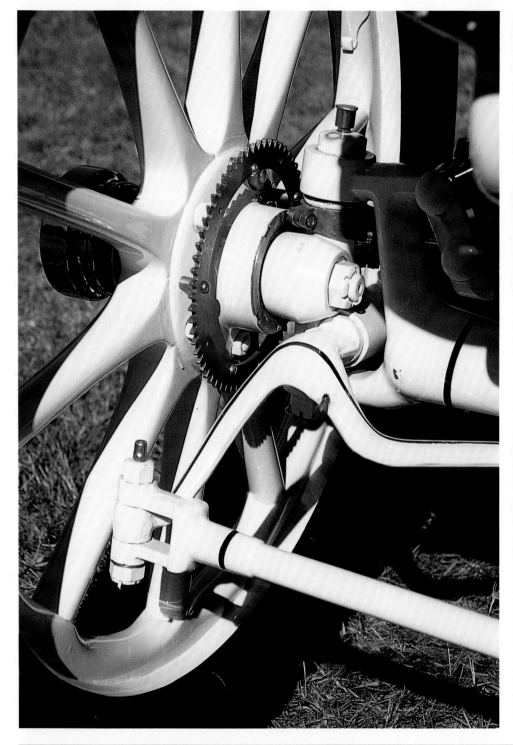

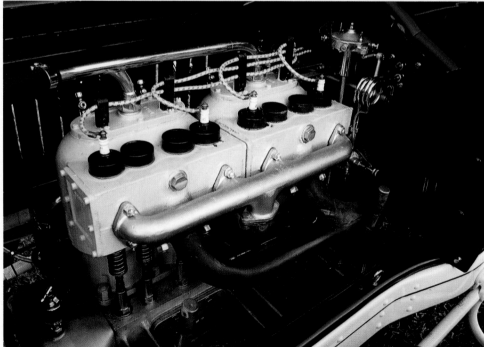

amateur historian and wrote a monograph on "Devon and Its Historic Surroundings," before the advent of the auto.

"It was a grand sight when the rattling old coach, with its foam-flecked horses and its eager passengers within and on top, dashed up to the door of the Roadside Inn," Hunter wrote in his picturesque vein. "There can be no question that our grandfathers enjoyed themselves in their own way, but in the advancement of the past half-century, their sons have come to look with something akin to pity on the meagreness of their facilities."

For all of his romantic leanings, Hunter himself came to look with pity on everything else after he bought his Packard. He considered it a sporting machine and entered it in two Pike's Peak Hill Climbs.

Though Hunter bought a new Packard Thirty in 1909, he did not neglect the Model N, and in 1922, a Philadelphia Packard dealer asked to borrow the N to display as a "Packard Still In The Service of the Original Owner." (At a tender age, it was an antique car.) Hunter's Packard was chosen because he maintained it carefully, and it still looked new. The dealer was so pleased to have such a car in his window that he ordered signs heralding it, one of which he nailed into the back of the Model N. Hunter was furious and snatched his car back to the safe haven of Devon.

When William Hunter died on board the *Vulcania* returning from Italy in 1933, the Model N showed about 50,000 miles, yet every piece of original hardware remained on the car. Mrs. Hunter told Ballard it had been driven to the West Coast several times, and Hunter's sons recalled escaping with it for moonlit runs, to 75 mph, on the local pike.

There can be no question that our grandfathers enjoyed themselves in their own way.

1912 Thirty Brougham

JOSIE O'DAY was a show-off—that is not her real name, but it will suffice. She was a denizen of Kansas City and a reflection of that city which is east to the West and west to the East.

While Mrs. O'Day's tastes were Fifth Avenue, her outlook was Cripple Creek. In 1912, a gentleman-admirer, who was a married man, gave her a Packard Thirty brougham. Thereafter, Mrs. O'Day drove the car through the streets of Kansas City, indiscreet, unashamed, and by no means unrewarded. She liked to wear big hats, too.

Two Packard brougham variations were offered in 1912: a single-compartment type and a double-compartment type, which was divided by glass and equipped with a telephone between the front and rear. Both were best-suited to city driving, but obviously, the double-compartment brougham was intended for people with chauffeurs and it was by far the more popular. In fact, no evidence exists to prove that more than one single-compartment brougham was ever built.

Mrs. O'Day, however, apparently liked to drive and yet stay unmussed. Her Thirty brougham cost $5500 and was constructed in aluminum by Packard, painted dark plum, as it is today. The glory of the interior was the black goatskin upholstery on the seats, door coves, and headliner. The goatskin survives to this day, showing its three-score and seventeen years and showing, too, the thick tufting and generous scope of Edwardian nicety.

The dark blue silk curtains and the grosgrain and brocade trim also speak of that long-gone era, when interior appointments of fine cars were copied from the parlors of fashion-

The Packard sales catalog for 1912 showed a new style, the brougham.

able homes. It is a credit to the former and current owners of the brougham that the interior has been left alone, for it is frankly irreplaceable.

"The Packard Motor Car Company is an organization of young men who have learned their business in Packard shops and driving Packard cars," explained the company's sales catalog for 1912. "For fourteen years this organization has devoted itself to producing cars exclusively of the highest type."

The same catalog described the complete line of three models, two in their last year of production—the Thirty and its city-bred little sibling, the Eighteen—and one in its first year—the Six.

The Thirty was Packard's most successful, and last, four-cylinder model, in production from 1907 to 1912. It was also the peak accomplishment in the tenure of Henry Joy as head of the Packard Motor Car Company, a position he held from 1903 to 1917. When he discovered Packard, by buying a Packard car in 1901, the company character was in place, but its product was practically homemade. By 1912, when the brougham was produced, the company had 33 acres of production space. Joy infused the company with his progressive spirit, best described by his own personal battle cry, "Do something, even if it's wrong." He wasn't an automobile man before he joined Packard, and he wasn't an

Owned by Marshall Mathews

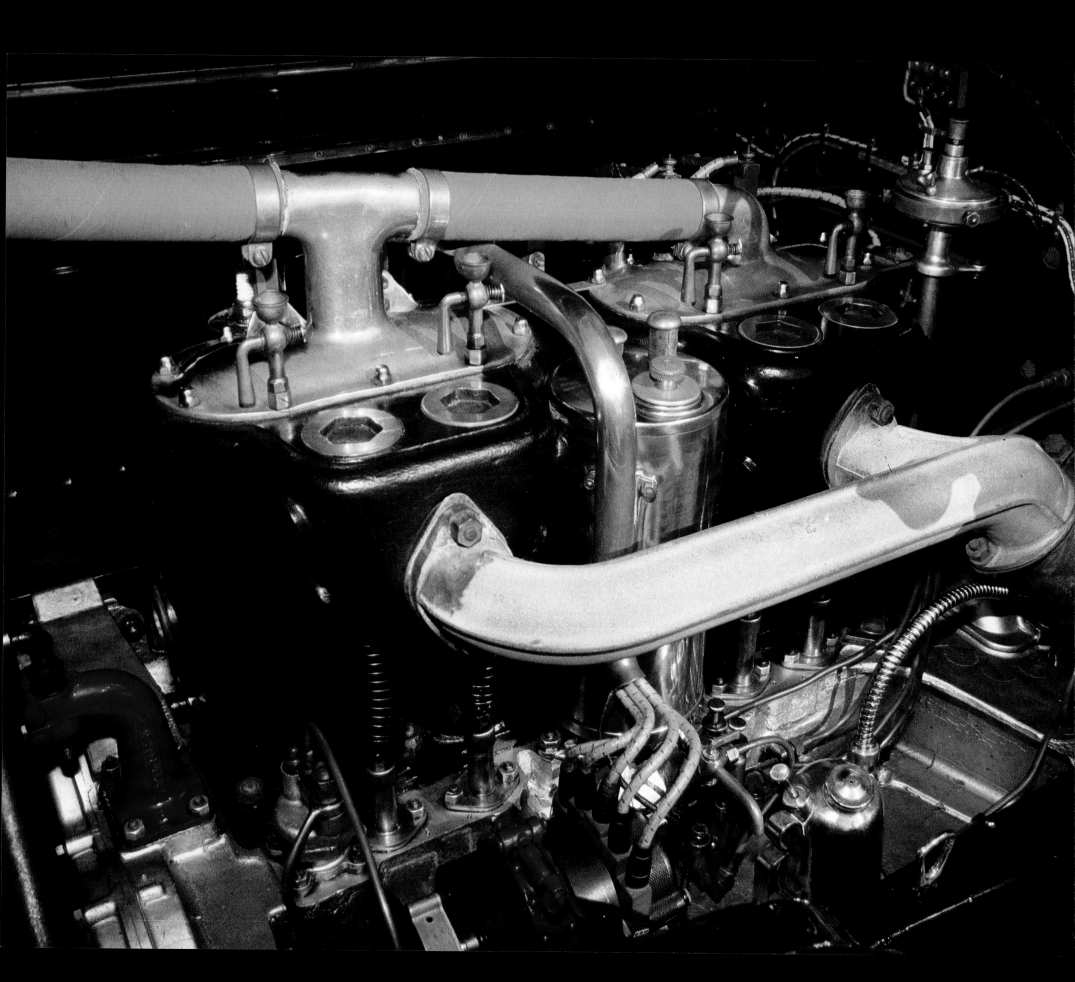

automobile man after he left the company: He learned his business in Packard shops and driving Packard cars.

When the Thirty debuted in 1907, its new engine was more sophisticated than that of its predecessor, the ''24,'' and it was stronger by six horsepower, at 30 hp. In 1912, a total of 1250 Model Thirty Packards were produced, augmenting the 8290 that were sold in four previous years.

The Thirty was well-known for its ease of operation, though Mrs. O'Day would have to have had a bit of a punch, as 1912 was the last year in which Packards were equipped with a crankstart. It was also Packard's last year for right-hand drive and gas headlamps. The current owner of the brougham, Marshall Mathews, claims it is more powerful than one would expect of such a heavy, four-cylinder car; many people who ought to know better assume it has a six-cylinder engine. ''A freeway ride is very surprising,'' he says.

"It just goes down the road straight as an arrow at 45 or 50 mph with no extra noises or rattles." A freeway ride in the brougham would be surprising indeed, least of all for the people in the brougham.

As a car of lines and shapes, the brougham is a veritable treatise on anti-aerodynamics.

In the year that Mrs. O'Day was given her Packard, Kansas City was said to be the most American city in the country: Eighty percent of its inhabitants were American-born. Men liked big-brimmed, black hats, and silver dollars were more common than paper money.

"All over Kansas City old buildings are coming down to make place for new ones; hills of clay are being gouged away and foundations dug; steel frames are shooting up," the writer Julian Street reported in 1913. "Looking upon these multifarious activities was like looking through an enormous magnifying glass at some gigantic ant hill, where thousands upon thousands of workers were rushing about, digging, carrying, constructing, all in breathless haste."

Every so often in that din of progress, Kansas City, 1913, a great, big, and dainty Packard brougham rolled through, with a woman at the wheel and a feather hat on her head, and then there was no hurry.

1913-14 Six, 1-38 Runabout

PACKARD MADE its first six-cylinder cars from 1912 to 1915, a short span in the history of the company but a major pivot in its fortunes nonetheless.

Franklin had made America's first practical six-cylinder engine in 1905. Chadwick produced its own splendid version in 1906, and thereupon began a debate among automakers on four cylinders versus six. "I am not a 'six-cylinder crank,'" Harry Lozier warned his chief engineer when the debate heated up at his factory. Peerless and Pierce-Arrow introduced gigantic six-cylinder cars in 1907, each producing 60 hp. The six gained favor rapidly with the motoring public, as it was believed to be quieter, stronger, faster, and snazzier. In addition, the enormous car bodies then in vogue seemed better suited to six-cylinder power. In 1907-08, Lozier, Alco, Thomas, Winton, and Stevens-Duryea all brought out six-cylinder models. These were the most expensive cars made in America, with sophisticated, precise machinery that more than proved the worth of the six.

During this rush, Packard stood firm with its excellent four-cylinder cars, the Eighteen and the Thirty, which were beautifully made and justifiably popular. They withstood comparison to the smaller Peerless and Pierce-Arrow sixes. And Packard could accept that.

However, in corporate identity, the other two automakers were gaining in prominence over Packard with their irreproachable sixes. The "Three Ps," as cast in 1910, seemed to place Peerless and Pierce-Arrow at the forefront, with Packard bringing up the rear. Packard could not accept that.

A Packard factory photograph of the 1914 1-38 Six runabout

Irving Berlin had a song hit called "Everybody's Doing It," in 1911, and to that tune, Packard brought out its first six-cylinder car. The company nicknamed it the "Dominant Six" and hoped that it would dominate its rivals.

The Six delivered 48 hp from a 525cid engine. In August 1912, a 38hp/414.7cid version was offered. Peerless and Pierce-Arrow, who often seemed to operate in tandem, also offered 38hp and 48hp models, and, of course, that invited comparison, then and now.

Packard's 48hp model had a topspeed of 70 mph, a figure only attained by the 60hp models from the other P-firms. In addition, the 48hp Packard delivered five more brake horsepower than Pierce's 48, an engine of the same size. Overall, the Packard distinguished itself among the three as the peppiest, with stiff acceleration from the standing start.

Having produced a successful six, the Packard Motor Car Company dropped its four after 1912, never to return to its former favorite. The Packard six that is featured here is a series 1-38, dating from 1913-14. The body was made in 1913, while the engine and chassis were built in 1914. It was in the initial series of 38hp models, and so it has the "1-" prefix. This series represented the first Packards equipped with electric headlights and an electric starter-generator. With just 24,000 miles, the phaeton runabout still has

Owned by Robert C. Robinson Sr.

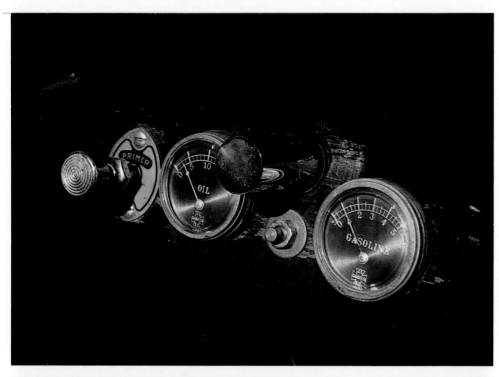

its original blue paint.

The Six opened a new era for Packard, but just as significantly, it closed one out, with the last hand-built Packard. To finish one took two months and required workers with 80 different trades. Two workers had the sole duty of going over each finished chassis to fill in scratches and to polish it to a glass-like fineness; a customer would never even see the chassis, normally.

In the dawning of the American six, companies simply spared no effort or expense. Alco, it is said, lost $425 on each of its $9000 cars. In the next round of competition, efficiency and labor costs that doubled overnight loomed formidably over such abject perfectionism.

The morning of the opulent American six was over.

1917 Twin Six, 2-25 Phaeton

A TWIN SIX PACKARD was a singular machine, and Harris Comings knew it. And he wanted his children to know it. "Prescott Hill is the steepest hill in Monterey County," his son Sherman said. "Dad went up that once in high gear just to show us kids what the Packard would do. It flew over."

There wasn't a hill in Monterey County, California, that the gray Twin Six wouldn't scale in high gear, a tribute to Jesse Vincent, Packard's vice president of Engineering and the mastermind behind the Twin Six. Its 100-percent increase in torque over previous, six-cylinder models was a source of particular satisfaction for him.

The Twin Six, introduced in 1915 and continued through 1923, was a phenomenal success for Packard, increasing sales, profits, company reputation, and capacities in engineering and production. Yet due to economies of scale, the Twin Six was less expensive than preceding Packard models.

Aside from increasing torque, one of Vincent's goals with the Twin Six was refining the Packard ride. It is a smooth mover, and it handles like a far lighter car. One of its most impressive feats—then or now—was its ability to slow to 3 mph and then accelerate to 60 mph, while remaining in high gear (a trait shared by the V-12 Packards of 1932-39).

The Packard Motor Car Company considered the V-12 engine its sovereign domain: Others might trespass but never surpass. The Twin Six broke the new ground for Packard, quietly and with a smug reserve of power.

Harris Comings on an outing with his aunt in Monterey County, California

Harris Comings' Twin Six phaeton was a Second Series model, with an improved engine of the same size as the First Series: 424 cid, producing 88 hp. The first owner was Clair Foster, a structural engineer who invented an advanced type of scaffolding in the earliest years of the century. By 1917, Foster was a 48-year-old squire, living in retirement on a farm in Great Barrington, Massachusetts. It was possibly there that he bought the Twin Six, and he may have been looking forward to using it in his gentle life on the Berkshire farm.

And again, he might not have been: When the United States entered World War I, Foster was called into the Army Corps of Engineers, and he embraced this second career with a vigor that suggests outright flight from the pastoral life.

After the war, Foster moved to Carmel, California, and took up his third career, as a pioneer in ham radio. He had a winning charm about him, and he made friends all over the world from his radio set. He and his wife soon came to realize that California could be a clammy place, so they replaced the Packard with a closed Wills Sainte Claire in 1928. Foster gave the Packard to his neighbor, Mr. Comings.

Comings was a jack-of-all-trades, one of which was car repair and another of which was bootleg liquor, which he ran out of his garage.

Owned by Marshall Mathews

He found the Packard Twin Six phaeton such a joy going up hills, but it could be a terror on the other side, going down. ''The car had only rear-wheel brakes, which made it tough going downhill on steep grades due to the heavy engine,'' his son Richard recalled.

''It was quite a car,'' Sherman added. ''But Dad thought it had bad points. It had a collapsible top, and if the weather got the least bit inclement, you'd have to put the top up, and that could take 20 minutes.'' The car still sports its original side curtains. ''And it was such a gas hog,'' Sherman continued. ''It didn't pay to take it on trips. When he took us to Yosemite, for instance, he used one of the old four-cylinder Wintons he had.''

In 1933, Harris Comings' financial situation forced the quick sale of the Twin Six, for $50, to a rancher named William Hatton. It has remained on the Monterey Peninsula ever since, unstoppable up hills—and down.

1920 Twin Six, 3-35 Rubay Roadster

LÉON RUBAY was born in 1870 in Paris, the transformed "City of Lights" to the rest of the world and "une ville ruisselante de lumiere," in the idiom of its denizens: "a city dripping with light." White stone palaces left over from the Second Empire shimmered under mile-long strings of glowing gaslight in clean air yet unbesmirched by autos or factories. "The undisputed social capital," said a frequent visitor to the Paris of Rubay's youth, "the equally undisputed capital of literature and art, the greatest pleasure-city of the world, she stood alone and without a rival."

Such a place at such a time leaves its own conceits upon its intimates, and Léon Rubay was a child of this Paris: artistic, uninhibited, and invincibly confident. He arrived in New York City in 1902 to sell French-made automobile accessories.

By 1915, Léon Rubay was a veteran of two New York coachbuilding companies and was appointed head of the pleasure-vehicle department of the White Company in Cleveland. Encouraged by the promise of contracts with White, Rubay formed his own coachbuilding company in 1916. Automotive styling was a new form of expression at this juncture, with few rules and guidelines that were leftover from Pullman cars and horse-and-buggy days. Custom coachwork of the mid-Teens is inconsistent and often awkward, but it has the excitement of a fresh pursuit, an art in its infancy. No one yet knew right from wrong: Enter an opinionated Frenchman.

As a new American and the president of the company,

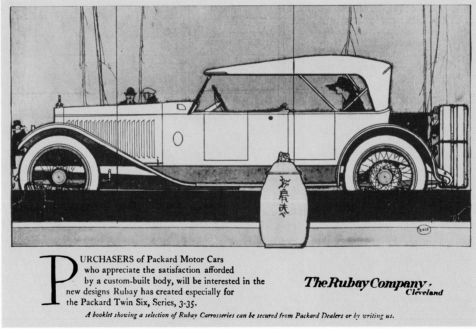

PURCHASERS of Packard Motor Cars who appreciate the satisfaction afforded by a custom-built body, will be interested in the new designs Rubay has created especially for the Packard Twin Six, Series, 3-35.

The Rubay Company, Cleveland

A booklet showing a selection of Rubay Carrosseries can be secured from Packard Dealers or by writing us.

A detail from a 1919 ad touting Rubay's line for the 3-35 Twin Six

Rubay offered a line of conventional body styles. As chief designer and a born-Parisian, he also made bodies that were like no others, derived not from last year's cars but from the entire world of nature, ideas, and invention.

If Picasso and Braque made Cubist paintings, Rubay made a Cubist car body, in sections of motion as he saw them in

his mind. He also made a car that looked like a dolphin, not as a Rose Bowl float is made to look like a dolphin, but in his perception of the form of a dolphin.

Léon Rubay was delighted by color and new paint formulations. One was a musty gray finish that was daubed on: To modern eyes, it made the car look as though it needed immediately to be painted, but at the time it was avant garde.

The White Company commissioned Rubay to produce all nine body styles for its advanced four-cylinder gasoline car, the "Sixteen-Valve 4." He also supplied bodies for the H.A.-Lozier, for Franklin, and later, for Model A Duesenbergs. Business was good, and Rubay hired young designers, including Thomas Hibbard and Ralph Roberts who each ran their own coachbuilding firms eventually. Like other coachbuilders in later generations, Rubay realized that Packard represented a ripe market. In 1919, his firm was an authorized Packard supplier, and a catalog of his designs was available through Packard dealers.

Owned by John and Perky King

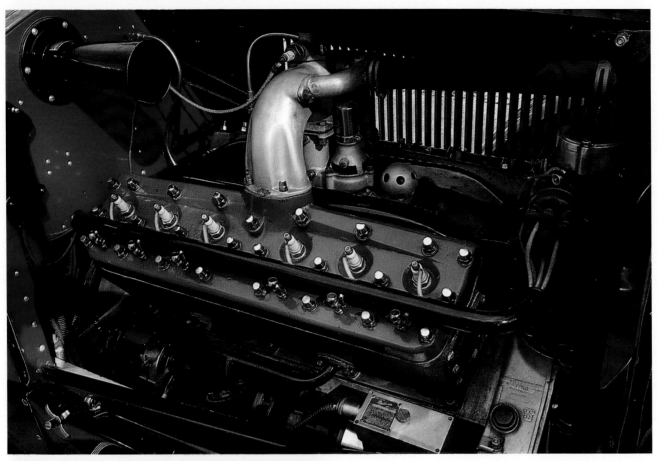

The catalog, ''Rubay Carrosserie Automobile for Packard Twin Six 3-35,'' depicted eight styles, most with names that referred to the French participation in World War I, from the ''Chateau Thierry'' five-passenger phaeton to the ''Marshall Foch'' field sedan. For Rubay, the bodies were subdued, sold as much on workmanship as on design. With none of the frolicsome musing of Rubay's earlier work, they were meant to ''enhance the satisfaction and pride discriminating people derive in the ownership of a Packard Twin Six.'' Rules were settling in, and Rubay was abiding by them.

The Packard Twin Six was in its third incarnation in 1919, the model 3-35. Its 12-cylinder engine, rated at 90 hp, was equipped with a patented Fuelizer, which preheated fuel in the intake manifold, for quieter running. An oilman in Oklahoma purchased a 3-35 Twin Six chassis in 1918 and had it sent to Rubay and Company in Cleveland to be fitted with the ''Ormonde'' roadster body from the catalog.

The standard Rubay roadster was a smooth silhouette,

somewhat lower than the Packard-body roadster. In the style of the day, one line runs across the car, hood to deck, interrupted but not broken by the passenger compartment.

The Oklahoman was apparently tall—about 6 feet 5 inches to judge from the placement of the seats in his roadster; they were set back to make more legroom, while the steering wheel was lengthened six inches and angled downward. To allow more headroom, and to echo the Packard look, the top was constructed in a style much more erect than the one normally supplied with Rubay roadsters.

Léon Rubay toyed with windshields on many of his designs, even managing a five-paneled cockpit on one body contemporary with the Packard roadster. On the roadster, he crafted a slanted windshield of three panes, all adjustable so that the driver could direct the wind.

In back of the seats, Rubay included two compartments, in one of which is the release for the rumble seat. The golf club trunk is accessible from either side, and the passenger door is specially fitted for golf balls, tees, and other accoutrements to what was more like a Twin Six Packard golf cart.

In his general catalog, Rubay noted that prices were based upon a chassis being delivered with fenders, running boards, and shields. Other Packard roadsters by Rubay employed the standard Packard flaring front fenders, and one is known to have had a step-plate in place of a running board, but on the Oklahoman's roadster, smaller fenders were incorporated, possibly at his request.

In 1920, Rubay's wife died, and he faltered. He took an extended stay in France and, on his return, organized a company to build a Léon Rubay car, which was advanced in many ways but did not succeed. His fellow Frenchman Georges Braque once said, ''Progress in art consists not in extending one's limits, but in knowing them better.'' By 1928, Rubay retreated to France again, worn down and worn out.

Classic Years
1921-1942

KING HENRY III of France visited Venice in 1574 and made a stop at the Arsenal, the city-state's navy yard. On his tour, he saw a warship in the first stage of construction: just ribs and a keel. After a two-hour break for a meal, Henry came back to find that the ship was finished, manned, and ready for active duty. The Arsenal was an assembly-line industrial complex with 16,000 employees. It could produce ships for trade or war at the rate of one per day, including every single item needed on board.

The philosophy of the Arsenal could have been the model for nearly any automaker in America in the Twenties. Its efficiency would have drawn envy from any of them.

Alfred Sloan, the president of General Motors, divided automobile history into three periods: the "class" market (when cars were for the rich) ending in 1908; the "mass" market (started by Henry Ford's Model T in 1908) lasting through the mid-Twenties, and the "class-mass" market (when better cars were produced in volume), which belonged to GM. In his 1964 book, *My Years with General Motors*, Sloan did not record that the last era ever did end. He wrote about four elements—installment selling, the used-car trade-in, the closed body, and the annual model—as factors that combined to allow and encourage middle-class customers to buy more new cars more often.

To Sloan, these conditions merely represented an opportunity for GM to surpass Ford. Packard, however, saw a new era coming, too, and considered that a mass-class market

You Can't Go Wrong IN A PACKARd

Ask the Girl Who Has Walked Home From One

was also a Packard market.

However, the company had to expand to greet the new mass-class era. The seeds of transformation lay with Alvan Macauley, the consummate businessman who became president of Packard in 1916. Macauley was educated and deliberate, very much like Sloan. He had overseen the volume

production of the popular Twin Six model starting in 1915, but in 1918, when Packard managed to produce 6500 Liberty engines for use in airplanes in World War I, his vision for the company began to hit stride. All previous lessons were applied to a new assembly line for the company's first postwar model, the Single Six in 1920. The pace continued unabating through the end of the decade.

Six thousand Packard cars were manufactured in 1920. In 1929, production was higher by a factor of eight, as 48,000 cars were made, and the company earned a record profit of $25 million. Figures fell in 1931-34, but by 1937, Packard had retrenched. One hundred ten thousand cars came off the line that year as the company focused on popular-priced models: the One Twenty and the Six, from 6000 to 110,000 cars in the same place on East Grand Boulevard in Detroit. Yet in Macauley's Packard company, accelerated production would never show in the basic quality of the product or in the serene facade of the corporation.

Inside the factory, however, accelerated production showed everywhere. To assembly-line workers, the dreaded word was "speed-up." A company could not enjoy an eight-times increase in production in just nine years, as had Packard—25 times in 17 years—without its foremen cranking up the line and calling out, "presto" (Italian); "mach schnell" (German); "putch-putch" (Polish): "hurry up."

Earlier auto workers were mostly mechanics and skilled machinists, employed at a variety of tasks, but by the mid-Twenties, 80 percent of workers at the factory had the same low skill level, according to *American Automobile Workers, 1900-1933*, by Joyce S. Peterson.

Among automakers, Packard was progressive in its attitude to the man on the line; *The Packard Advanced Training School* manual for foremen, issued in 1919, forbade attempts to "intimidate the workmen," encouraging appeals to the workman's "sense of honor." Still, by honor or intimidation, the line had to move faster and faster.

In 1929, during one of Packard's best and busiest years, *The Nation* published the experiences of a worker at Packard, Robert L. Cruden. Cruden often reported on conditions at American factories from the viewpoint of the worker. He had been hired at Packard as a ventilator assembler:

" 'No loitering. Get out Production.' This sign on our general foreman's desk symbolized the whole system. Our job was to put ventilators into bodies as they came along on the 'line.' We had to work swiftly, for if a body went through unassembled there was trouble and plenty of it. We would receive a visit from the general foreman, after which all would speed until our shirts stuck to our bodies. But then the jobs would not be well done and another visit would result. It

was an impossible situation: the output was increased almost daily but no one was added to our 'gang.'

"We worked eleven hours a day; we were ready to quit after seven. After five in the afternoon we would . . . work away in a semi-conscious state. . . . It was even worse, I think, with the 'wet sanders' who help polish the glistening Packard bodies. Their job consists of rubbing the Duco lacquer with wet, very fine sandpaper. In order to get results they have to concentrate all their energy in their hands. At about 2:30 in the afternoon they begin to weaken. Sweat streams from their faces, their arms move slower and slower, forced on by sheer will power and fear of the boss. Ill temper and mutual abuse increase with their fatigue.

"Several times I went down to the main spraying room. In that department spraying booths and baking ovens alternate, so that with spray and stale hot air, the atmosphere in the room is suffocating. Each time I went down I was driven out after a few minutes, lung-sore and choking. The sprayers there work in their underwear, the poisonous spray easily penetrating their pores. These men are supposed to wear little aluminum respirators, but few of them do. 'Hell,' one of them said to me, 'we'd choke to death with one of them on.' Going home one night I talked with an old sprayer who had been a long time with the company, about the effect of this on his lungs. 'Buddy,' he responded, 'they're sore. Some nights I can hardly sleep. But what can I do?'

"Last summer Packard proudly announced that 'economies in production' would allow for a $300 cut in the price of cars. The workers partook of these economies by accepting wage cuts."

In 1937, the Packard Motor Car Company recognized the

United Automobile Workers Union without resistance. Further troubles, however, were in store on the floor of the factory. In 1943, black workers at Packard protested that they were not being promoted regularly; When a handful were given better jobs, 25,000 white workers walked out on the spot. The U.A.W. blamed Packard's troubles on Ku Klux Klan agitators; the National Association for the Advancement of Colored People blamed Packard management, and Packard itself blamed wartime conditions, "thin supervision" over a teeming workforce that included too many people without factory experience.

Between the wars, Packard enjoyed hard-won success and saw the demise of many of its old rivals: Peerless (1932); Marmon (1933); Franklin (1934); Stutz (1935); Duesenberg (1937), and Pierce-Arrow (1938). Packard changed in response to contrary conditions, and by 1940, it was very different from the company it had been in 1920.

Before his first day at Packard in 1928, a worker named Clayton Fountain couldn't get to sleep, he was so excited. "Each time I closed my eyes," he later wrote, "visions of hundred-dollar paychecks danced in front of them. Daydreams of new suits and Saturday nights with a pocketful of dough to spend in the speakeasies floated through my mind." Payday was the dream of the auto worker, because wages were better than the national average. At the Arsenal in Venice, three hundred years before, payday was a city-wide holiday.

"We tore around all night in automobiles," Fountain wrote of his early life at Packard, "speeding from one blind pig to another, banging away on ukeleles and singing such tunes as 'Me and the Man in the Moon' at the top of our voices."

1925 Eight, 243 Touring Car

"LET ME SAY that it was 19 years after I was married before I had a whole "day off" by myself without a member of my family," Mary Henry wrote in 1950. "No one appreciated this long term of home duty more than my husband did and he showed his appreciation by saying, 'Go to it and go to all the places and do all the things you want to do and I believe are well fitted to do. You have earned it and I will help in every way I can.' He was even better than his word. He supplied me with a car and a chauffeur, Ernest Perks, who is now gardener, and who, after 21 years, continues to drive me on my trips."

Perks would drive Mrs. Henry on her journeys until the year of her death, 1967. "Mrs. Henry was the most famous botanist in the United States," he recalled, "and we covered every state then, mostly on back roads. The first car we drove was the Henrys' Packard touring car. The only thing I wouldn't do with that car was go over little backroad bridges; I was nervous because the car weighed so much."

Dr. J. Norman Henry bought the car in 1925 because he needed something commodious to carry himself, his wife, Mary, their five children, the baggage, and their pet police dog, who rode behind a rack on the running board. The family lived outside of Philadelphia but traveled frequently to their farm in Maryland. Previously a Peerless customer, Dr. Henry settled on the Packard Straight Eight touring car, with its length of 17 feet 4 inches.

It was car enough for the Henry family in terms of space. And in terms of time—the passing of years—it was car

With Ernest Perks at the wheel, Mrs. Mary Henry in her Packard touring car

enough, too, for they never stopped using it.

After 1928, Mary Henry used the Packard on her scientific expeditions around North America, and in 1935, the Henrys' son, Howard, took it to college. He still owns the car.

"The touring is great to drive and remarkably easy to steer, for such a large, heavy car," Howard Henry said. "Unfor-

tunately, the brakes are not nearly as effective as modern brakes, though they were among the first four-wheel, mechanical brakes."

Except for the low-production Duesenberg Model A (which was even more advanced with *hydraulic* four-wheel brakes) and small concerns like Rubay, Packard was the first to announce four-wheel brakes, in 1923. Previous to the Packard announcement, automakers considered the four-wheel system a great idea but one that American customers would never accept. Packard was in a different position than almost every other company, though: When it assured the public that four-wheel brakes were all right, all doubts vanished.

"The Packard Second Series Straight Eight engine has nine main bearings, which makes it ultra-smooth and quiet running," Henry continued. "Although it sits for long periods of time without running, it has been consistently easy to start." The 358cid L-head Eight produces 85 hp.

In 1925, two young men drove an identical model all the

Owned by Howard G. Henry

way across the country and started it just once, at the outset in Los Angeles. In fact, they never even stopped the forward motion of the car. They had a special rolling jack for changing tires and one of the two taught himself to attach and detach tire chains on the moving car.

Dr. and Mrs. Henry bought their Model 243 before that durability run. Dr. Henry was a physician with special expertise and influence in areas of public health, such as pure drinking water and the treatment accorded mental health patients. He was also a true anglophile and was the captain of a Philadelphia cricket team.

Mrs. Henry, with nothing more in the way of a formal education than her high school diploma, was cited by the Royal Horticultural Society in 1947 as ''having discovered more new plants in the United States than anyone else.'' According to the University of Pennsylvania, this amounted

to more than 50 new plants. She stored specimen plants behind the rack on the Packard running board. In Georgia once, Perks was digging a plant when some moonshiners mistook him for a Treasury agent. After that, he gave up his chauffeur's cap.

Mrs. Henry took 11 trips through the Rocky Mountains, and in 1931, the Canadian government named a Rocky after her, Mt. Mary Henry. Located just north of 58th parallel, it is 9292 feet high. Her findings on geographical matters aided in the construction of the Alaskan Highway as a wartime supply line in 1942.

The Henrys' Packard was equipped with an optional heater that was built into the floor, to channel engine exhaust under the passengers' feet in winter. There was also an interchangeable, closed body for cold weather. Notwithstanding, Mrs. Henry retired the car in 1933 for a Packard sedan.

In 1935, Howard Henry was ready to go off to college at Penn. "My parents didn't seem to be in a position to buy me a new car," he said, "so my father offered me the '25 Packard touring." He opted at that time to paint over the original Packard blue, to dark gray with red stripes and monogrammed doors—something befitting a college freshman.

After the war, Henry purchased his family's farm in Maryland. He stashed the Packard touring car in a barn until he began to appreciate it as an antique. It has never been restored, and the engine has been overhauled only once, in 1973. In 1960, the touring car played the part of Franklin D. Roosevelt's Packard in the movie *Sunrise At Campobello*. At that time, the top was put down for the first time ever.

In June of 1925, Dr. Henry bought a car for his family, and a car for his family is just what it turned out to be.

1926 Eight, 243
Dietrich Convertible Coupe

RAY DIETRICH was a dreamy sort of designer who could sweeten the look of a car with gentle curves placed just so against one another. He was also a pretty tough kid from the Bronx.

Alvan Macauley, the president of Packard, was a dour businessman, but he liked to hover over the drawing boards in the company design rooms, voicing his own opinions. Throughout the spring of 1926, Mr. Macauley was the prey, and Ray Dietrich was the hunter.

Dietrich began his career with Brewster in New York, and in 1920, he founded LeBaron there with Tom Hibbard and Ralph Roberts soon after. Hibbard left subsequently to work in Paris, but LeBaron was such a soaring success that Edsel Ford tried to move the whole company to Detroit. However, no one at the firm wanted to trade the swank salons of New York for the smoke stacks of Detroit. Except Dietrich. After an unpleasant parting from LeBaron, he set up shop in Detroit and set his sights on Macauley.

Dietrich wanted his Packard designs to be sold through Packard dealerships and illustrated in the general sales catalog. Macauley flatly refused. Such an arrangement involved Packard in a risk that he felt should be Dietrich's own. Dietrich took the case, as it were, to the dealers themselves. He built three Packards—a convertible coupe, a convertible sedan, and a sport sedan—and he showed them on a glitzy tour across the country, to New York, Boston, Washington, St. Louis, Chicago, Los Angeles, and San Francisco. These private exhibitions were held in hotel lobbies, and as often

A convertible coupe on Dietrich's posh hotel tour in 1926

as possible, the cars were also parked outside on the sidewalk. The Dietrich look was expressed by a phrase Dietrich himself used in an article for *The Classic Car*, when he noted that a designer would look for "the flowing line of least resistance."

Hundreds of individual orders flooded the home office.

Meanwhile, dealers were incited to a fever—a fever that swept East Grand Boulevard in the form of 175 orders for factory Dietrich-Packards. Two months later, Macauley surrendered himself voluntarily to Dietrich's office, and a contract was signed.

Perhaps John Ridge, a paving contractor from Sterling, Illinois, was present for the initial Dietrich exhibit in Chicago. In any case, he was in the first wave of Dietrich-Packard customers in 1926, purchasing a dark blue convertible coupe. According to a workman's chalk mark later discovered under the upholstery, the car was built in April 1926. It was a Straight Eight on the Series 243 chassis; Ridge kept it until he died in 1956.

Like other custom cars of the mid-Twenties, the Dietrich convertible coupe actively resisted the high, narrow stance that was preponderent in cars of the day. It sits lower than the standard Packard, and the body bows out at the midsection to discourage a spindly appearance.

L. Morgan Yost purchased the convertible coupe from John

Owned by L. Morgan Yost

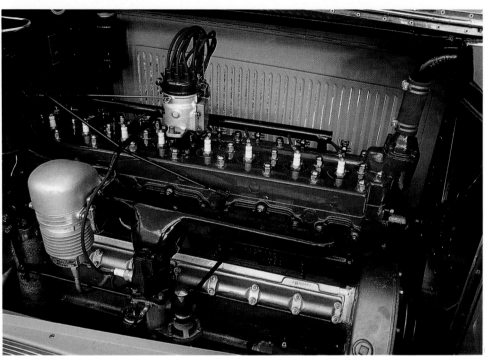

Ridge's estate in 1956 and decided to change the color to tarragon green, copying some chips of original paint found under the fender of a 1933 Dietrich-Packard.

Ray Dietrich continued as a design consultant with Packard through 1935 (his design for a 1934 convertible sedan is also featured in this book). He was influential at Studebaker, Dodge, Lincoln, Cadillac, and Pierce-Arrow as well.

As the first custom coachbuilder to take Detroit seriously, Dietrich was part of a revolution in auto styling and, more important, in the prevailing attitude toward styling. Ralph Roberts recognized it, too, and wrote in 1925, ''there is [currently] a special gratification for those who have always maintained that even an object as mechanical as the automobile may be treated in the delicate manner of the artist.''

For Dietrich, the gratification came quickly, and amazingly enough, it came in Detroit.

1926 Eight, 243 LeBaron Landaulet

IN THE SUMMER OF 1913, Glenn Stewart was between postings in the diplomatic corps, so he booked passage on a pleasure cruise of the Great Lakes. He was 29 years old, handsome, rich, and glib, and the young ladies onboard thought him terribly glamorous. He thought himself glamorous, too, and regaled them with stories of his overseas career, including the duel which resulted in the black patch that he wore over one eye.

One of those that Stewart met that summer was a Vassar sophomore who gushed a bit when she told her college roommate about "The Count," as Stewart was known aboard the ship. The roommate happened to be a cousin of Stewart's, and she knew him when—when he didn't have a black eye patch, among other things. "He's a liar, a womanizer, and a 'no account,' " she said. Perhaps he was, but 75 years later, Stewart was still vivid in the memory of his friend from Vassar, his friend of a few days on a Great Lakes cruiser.

Glenn Stewart was born in January 1884, in Pittsburgh, to a family with interests in banking and the grain trade. At Yale (class of '08), he stayed away from extra-curricular activities and away from certain of his classmates, too, for his yearbook epithet noted that, "his bark is worse than his bite." And his bite could be ferocious. According to the book, *Wye Island* by Boyd Gibbons, Stewart actually hurt his eye while at Yale, when a bomb he was planting detonated prematurely. He was planning to blow up the railroad tracks leading out of New Haven to keep a bevie of his favorite girls from leaving for an out-of-town party.

In the foreign service, Stewart was posted at Cuba, Gua-

Mrs. Jacqueline Archer Stewart with her Packard, in Washington, D. C.

temala, and South America before reporting to Vienna, Austria, as First Secretary just before World War I. His first wife, Greta, died in 1918, after just four years of marriage, and left him a fortune. In 1920, he was wed to the vivacious Jacqueline Archer. The same year, he retired from the diplomatic corps, reasoning that he was primarily interested in

world travel, and he could pursue that without the government. To celebrate, he and Jacqueline embarked upon a year-long wedding trip around the world.

The second Mrs. Stewart was an Irish heiress who had been raised on Indian reservations around America, her father, Lord Archer, having been a missionary. She was a dog breeder of repute and was so proud of some of her wolfhounds that, at their deaths, she had them stuffed and sent for display at the Museum of Natural History in New York.

The Stewarts were indulgent, attractive, alert, and certainly eccentric—for international social figures of the day, they were about par.

For the town of Easton, Maryland, they were fantastic. They settled on the Eastern Shore in 1922, moving into a castle patterned after the Alhambra in Spain and intended to be as secure. Stewart had an abiding fear of attack, and the castle was surrounded by a wire fence and patrolled by armed horsemen. Within the castle, he installed an iron gate that would lower each night

Owned by Howard G. Henry

over his bedroom.

Glenn Stewart was obsessed with travel. In 1928, he commissioned the nation's first motorhome, a "Flatavan," built on a Reo chassis, with four rooms, which he used on hunting trips in the Rockies. In addition to yearly trips to Europe and beyond, he became a yachtsman and explorer. He published an article in *American Geographical Quarterly* in 1932 about a trip through the Caribbean on which, using Christopher Columbus' journal, he followed "the discoverer's course step by step in a small boat."

In 1926, the Stewarts ordered a Packard limousine, to be used in Maryland and on their European trips in 1927 and 1929. The chassis was a Straight Eight Series 243, and the coachwork was entrusted to LeBaron. The six-year-old LeBaron company commanded the styling leadership of the East coast, the fresh talents of founders Ray Dietrich and Tom Hibbard eclipsing established coachbuilding companies like Brewster. The Stewarts' Packard was a landaulet, and it represented a combination of LeBaron's styling priorities and the Stewarts' fetish for privacy.

The nickel-plated hood of the Stewarts' Packard gave it a European air, more likely on a Rolls-Royce or Isotta Fraschini. The vee-shaped crease, or "raised panel," running from the radiator shell down the hood and across the painted

cowl to the windshield posts was a LeBaron innovation seen on the Minervas built under the Paul Ostruk badge and later on Duesenbergs of European design. Because the cabin of the car had to be raised to accommodate the Stewarts' interior appointments, the hood and the radiator were raised four inches. To compensate, that amount of metal was added to the bottom of the hood on either side and painted.

The late Hugo Pfau, a young designer at LeBaron in 1926, recalled working on the car when he examined it in 1973. He noted the different material covering the stationary and folding parts of the roof. This arrangement allowed the Stewarts to put chairs on the roof during polo matches.

The Packard's interior appointments also reflected the Stewarts' tastes . . . and needs. As the manager of the bank in Easton recalled, ''The bank came to Mrs. Stewart, not Mrs. Stewart to the bank.'' When the Packard pulled up in front of the bank, a teller would bring money out to Mrs. Stewart and conduct her transactions. In effect, the Packard had to be a rolling strong box for such errands and for the reserves of cash and jewels with which the Stewarts traveled. Under the back seat is a secret jewelry safe, and in the divider are two more hidden compartments. The single jump seat faces not forward but outward to the right. This was a place for Mrs. Stewart's ever-present dog, and it allowed more legroom for Mr. Stewart, who stood 6 feet 4 inches.

In 1929, the Stewarts replaced the Packard with a Duesenberg, which they used on their travels in the early Thirties. They were divorced in the Forties, and Glenn Stewart moved to Florida, where he died in 1957. Both the Duesenberg and the Packard were still in the castle garages when Mrs. Stewart died in 1964.

The Packard, like Glenn Stewart himself, demanded attention and disdained it in the same stroke, Americans both, long in the company of the aristocracy of Europe.

1927 Eight, 343
Murphy Convertible Sedan

CLAIR SUSSEX FAIRBANK was a widow in the Twenties with a house near the ocean in Morro Bay, California. She had four sons, and they liked to take constitutional walks in the open air. Mrs. Fairbank also had a taste for cars, in the recollection of another resident of Morro Bay—big, snazzy foreign cars.

When Mrs. Fairbank decided to try a big, snazzy American car in April 1927, she picked a Packard Eight, on the 143-inch wheelbase. Being a modish Californian, she chose a car with custom coachwork by the Walter M. Murphy Company of Pasadena, purchasing the finished product from a Packard dealer in Santa Ana. The Murphy look was sporty but solid. Fittingly, more J-Duesenbergs were bodied by Murphy than any other coachbuilder.

In 1927, however, the prospect of the J-Duesenberg was just column-filler for the auto pages. Murphy built three convertible sedans on Packard chassis that year, one for a banker, one for the movie actor Jack Holt, and one in cream with a brown leather interior for Mrs. Fairbank. The cost of the Fairbank car was $9180—which was $4000 more than the most expensive factory-bodied Packard of the year. It is the only one of the trio known to have survived.

Strother MacMinn, automobile designer, design teacher, and author, grew up near the Murphy factory in Pasadena and has made a thoughtful study of the company. "The convertible sedan style was a mainstay with Murphy," according to MacMinn, "and evolved from analysis and improvement of a style originated by Gangloff [the French-

Murphy's prototype convertible sedan, photographed in California.

Alsatian coachbuilder that supplied many distinctive bodies for Ettore Bugatti]. In this style, the doors are hinged at the center pillar and have no off-set for a wind-seal, thus permitting the side glasses to rise very close to the pillar and making the pillar itself very thin. (That is, the visible pillar above the beltline, between the side glasses.)

"The cast bronze windshield pillar was also very thin," MacMinn further explained, "giving unimpeded visibility and a light look to the whole upper. Murphy began building this style about 1927 and applied it to Rolls-Royce, Hispano-Suiza, and Hudson, as well as Packard—also as prototypes for Hudson and Auburn. The same basic architecture was also used to evolve hardtop sedans and town cars, as well as convertible sedans, on Duesenbergs."

Mrs. Fairbank was driven in her Packard by the family chauffeur, whose name happened to be Mr. Moto. In the Thirties, she married a Canadian, and from Morro Bay, she moved to a town called Petrolia in Ontario, just down the pike from Oil City and Oil Springs. To judge from the thick deposits of oil and the loose rivets that were later removed from the undercarriage of the Packard, it toured the oil fields of Petrolia extensively.

One of the Fairbank boys brought the Packard back to California. He sold it at one point, bought it back for $50, and

Owned by Phil and Alma Hill

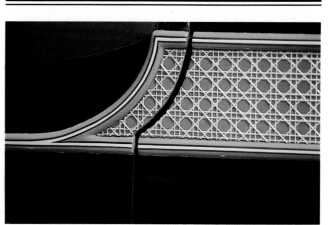

finally sold it again, in 1969, to Phil Hill, the race driver who was then forming the automobile restoration company Hill & Vaughn. Hill worked on the Packard by himself, mostly in his garage at home.

Hill made his name driving Ferraris and other race cars, but Packards run even deeper with him. When he was born, he was brought home from the hospital in his aunt's Packard roadster, and in 1941, he talked the same aunt into buying a Packard convertible victoria by Bohman & Schwartz like the one featured in this book.

"The convertible sedan is very nice to drive," Hill said. "But the Eight was supposed to be a big jump over the Twin Six; I'm not so sure it was. Four-wheel-brakes, introduced in 1924, were enormously superior to two, but to me, the use of balloon tires in 1925 was a questionable step. The ride is not sufficiently better to justify the low steering ratios that came with them. To turn, you have to go 'round and 'round. Power steering should have come along at the same time as low-pressure tires, but it didn't. The fact is, back in the Teens and early Twenties, you had more directional control."

Hill chose the purple color scheme of the Murphy Packard after seeing just such hues on another car from the same era. It has caused a stir in the galleries at concours events, as it probably would have jogged placid Morro Bay in 1927. But it might just have brightened Petrolia a bit.

1928 Six, 526 Standard Sedan

CHRISTMASTIME in Brooklyn in 1927 was windy and white. The place was a bustling borough of 2,169,210 people, although to avoid a potentially treacherous comparison with its high-stepping neighbor of Manhattan, it labelled itself "the city of homes and churches."

Big things may have happened in Manhattan, but many, many little things happened in Brooklyn. At Christmastime 1927, a plot was afoot in Rockaway Park, where a family named Geronimo lived in a chunky white stucco house only a few years old. The house had a wrap-around porch and rows of square pillars. It also had a yard not much bigger than a welcome mat and a garage in the back for one car.

Mr. Geronimo had provided a fine home for his family in a respectable part of town, but he wanted one more thing, aside, probably, from playing centerfield for the Dodgers. He wanted a Packard. The previous year, 34,391 people had purchased Packards, and Geronimo hadn't been one of them. In 1927, Mrs. Geronimo gave him one for Christmas.

The model that she picked out reflected the inclinations of a family man: a five-passenger sedan. That it was on Packard's Fifth Series Straight Six chassis may have been a practical consideration for people who lived in the city, or again, it may have been a practical consideration for a woman who could spend $2285 for a Six and not $4450 for the Straight Eight. The following year, Packard reduced the price of the Geronimo's sedan to $1985, as it closed out production of the Straight Six, placing it $10 away from the honor of being

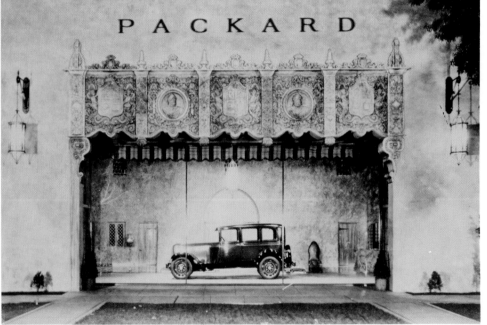

A 1928 standard sedan in the window of Packard-Brooklyn

the cheapest Packard of the year, of the Twenties, and of the company's history to date. Even at full price, however, the Fifth Series Packard Six was a good deal.

The Straight Six was introduced as the Single Six in 1920, Packard's entry in high-volume production. However, it took several years before production of the model would be termed "high."

The Six was supposed to be manageable, fuel-efficient, and reasonably priced, in addition to being smooth and quiet (like all good Packards). The Straight Six engine was an L-head, and when it finished its days in the Fifth Series, it displaced 288.6 cubic inches and produced 81 hp.

The stewardship of the Six was the responsibility of Alvan Macauley, who had been named president of the company in 1917. When the model faltered at the start, he did not abandon it and retreat to the expensive, and profitable, Twin Six. He determined that the Six needed a longer wheelbase and crisper styling, and he raised the money to effect the changes at the right time and without the company losing face. When the Twin Six reached the end of its production life in 1922, he replaced it with the Straight Eight, which was developed along the lines of the Six. The transitions were themselves Packard smooth and quiet.

The sedan that Mr. Geronimo received for Christmas was

Owned by Joseph J. Hossbacher, D.D.S.

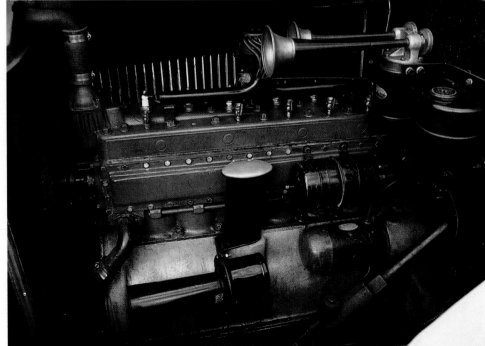

painted chickle drab, a sober color that settles well next to the standard black fenders and the canvas-covered spare tires. The paint and upholstery on the sedan are still original and, as the car has spent all but a fraction of its life in garages, have not been subject to fading from sunlight.

Joseph Hossbacher bought the Packard sedan in 1962 from the Geronimo family. ''When I was driving it home from their house,'' he recalled of that summer day in the city, ''I stopped at a tire dealer in Rockaway Park. A very old man came out to see the car. He told me he remembered when he had mounted the double-whitewall, Dayton Thoroughbred tires that were on the Packard.'' Not everyone would spring for double whitewall tires for a Packard Six sedan.

Geronimo only used his Packard on special occasions, mostly on outings with his family. In 32 years, the Geronimo family drove it but 12,000 miles. Most of the time, it was in the garage in back of the house, but as long as Mr. Geronimo knew it was there, it was earning its keep.

1929 Speedster, 626 Runabout

EMIL FIKAR was not exactly a gangster, but he did live in Chicago in the Twenties. And he did sell a prohibited beverage, and he did require a car that would outrun anything a sheriff might drive.

Fikar was a brewer, and during Prohibition, he produced near-beer, also known as "3.2" beer to denote its alcohol content. It may have been low in alcohol, but it was illegal just the same.

Early in 1928, Fikar walked into Buresch Motor Sales on Ogden Avenue in Chicago and asked about the new Packard speedster, the 626 model. In its advertising, Packard had dedicated the 626 to "the select few who frankly love the hum of racing car power throbbing to be unleashed at a toe-touch." (This may or may not recall the essential Emil Fikar.)

American automakers offered a burgeoning range of racing-car power in 1928-29. The mantle worn by the Stutz Black Hawk was about to be assumed by the Auburn speedster, while the Jordan Playboy, the Kissel White Eagle speedster, and the Chrysler Imperial were legitimate choices as well. Fikar may have been skeptical: He may have wondered if this new Packard speedster would turn out to be a sane, reliable, sober Packard sheathed in country-club bodywork.

In fact, Fikar was skeptical. According to the company's program, though, all 626 speedsters would be built to order, and none were displayed in showrooms. Fikar told Buresch that he would order the speedster out of the catalog, with its promised topspeed of 95 to 100 mph, but he stipulated that it had to be actually capable of 100 mph . . . or else. He was probably just enough of a Chicago gangster to give the

Fikar took this picture of his speedster the day he brought it home, October 6, 1928.

words "or else" a certain ring.

Buresch ordered the speedster, and Packard built it, and in the autumn, Buresch and Fikar traveled together to the Packard Proving Grounds, just north of Detroit. What they found there may have been just as impressive as the first sight of the new speedster; the Proving Grounds featured a

2½-mile oval track neatly landscaped and augmented with a brand new garage and a lodge for hospitality. It had opened just months before, in June 1928.

Fikar's speedster was driven out onto the track, subdued in gunmetal gray as ordered. According to Buresch, recalling the day 31 years later, the speedster topped out at 110 mph. Fikar accepted delivery of it, paying the $5000 base price and extra for two options: chromium-plated wire wheels ($250) and the deluxe hood ornament ($10).

Back in Chicago, Fikar took the speedster home on October 6, 1928. Its throaty exhaust, tremendous power and agility, and race-car proportions put it alone, even among Packards. Fikar was so pleased that he snapped a photograph of it in front of his house that same day.

The speedster itself may not have been conservative, but the Packard company's approach to it was. The 626 arrived at its level of performance through a few, highly effective changes to a Series 640 Custom Eight chassis.

The Custom Eight engine was fitted with a high-compression cylinder head and a high-lift camshaft, which raised the output from 106 bhp at 3200 rpm to 130 bhp. The voracious fuel consumption of the 626 speedster would be satiated by a vacuum pump drawing from a special 28-gallon tank. On the other end of the system, a muffler cutout was included to increase efficiency at high engine speeds.

In addition to the removal of 14 inches from the chassis, the rear axle ratio was reduced from 4.07 to 1 (for the Custom Eight roadster) to 3.3 to 1 for the 626 speedster. On the body, the 14 inches were missing from the rear end of the car, where the golf-club compartment would normally have gone. The result was that the engine compartment took up half of the 126½-inch wheelbase. The two seats were pushed back

overall, granting the car a long, racecar hood and guaranteeing that no one with long legs would take to the rumble seat voluntarily.

Only 74 speedsters were sold on the 626 chassis; all but a few were ordered with the rumble-seat roadster body, as opposed to a five-seat phaeton style that was also offered. At present, only one 626 is known to have survived: Emil Fikar's speedster-roadster, now owned by the Henry Ford Museum and Greenfield Village in Dearborn, Michigan.

The previous owner, Montgomery Young, had lived in Lake Forest, Illinois, for 30 years without hearing of the car. When a friend brought him to look at it in July 1959, it was in an old garage, covered with dust. Young bought it, over the objections of acquaintances who assured him that Packard had never built a car with such a big engine compartment and such a small wheelbase.

Young was inclined to believe them until he noticed the name of the dealer on the identification plate on the firewall. Buresch Motor Sales was still doing business in 1959, and

Mr. Buresch remembered the car immediately. He even located the original bill of sale. ''My Packard had turned out to be a one-in-a-million speedster-roadster,'' Young said, savoring a one-in-a-million pleasant surprise.

The new intelligence on the car inspired Young to restore it to original condition. Five thousand man-hours later, in March of 1966, he was finished. ''I have been interested in cars since the day I was born,'' he said. ''But the 626 has to be the most exciting car I ever drove. It wants to go, so you have to remember to slow it down all the time.''

In 1976, Young decided to find a new owner for the speedster. He donated it to the Henry Ford Museum, where it has been on display since 1978. It is never run anymore, and it has been drained of most engine fluids to discourage corrosion. As part of the exhibit, ''The Automobile in American Life,'' it sits perfectly still, not 30 miles from the site of the old Proving Grounds.

Now it sits still, but if it couldn't go 100 mph . . . 105 . . . 110, it never would have left Detroit. And it did.

1930 Deluxe Eight, 745
Waterhouse Convertible Victoria

PACKARD DEVELOPED a chassis in 1928 that was specifically intended as a dolly for custom coachwork: the 645, a 145-inch wheelbase version of the Sixth Series Deluxe Eight, normally 140 inches. The longer wheelbase had real appeal for coachbuilders and their customers: The man behind it was none other than Ray Dietrich, who had been retained by the company to design a custom-car series. In 1929, the Seventh Series Packard continued the 145-inch chassis, with provision for the engine to be mounted in a forward position (for more cabin room), or back by five inches (for a longer hood). This chassis, the 745, was the coachbuilder's Packard of its day, and that day was the peak of the coachbuilding business.

In Europe, a Russian émigré named Alexis de Sakhnoffsky was making a terrific impact with a special Packard design that he had created for the Belgian firm of Van den Plas, winning the 1929 Grand Prix de Monte Carlo Concours d'Elegance. His new design combined the attributes of a roadster with those of a coupe in a five-seat open car, the convertible victoria: "a car which can be quickly converted from a dashing open tourer into a chummy enclosed victoria," according to a salon catalog. It was fluid and at the same time substantial; it was sporty and elegant; it was a town-and-country car; it was an instant hit.

And it was a Packard, on the 645 chassis. Word of the new style filtered back to Detroit, and Packard decided to show a convertible victoria on a 745 chassis at the 1930 Paris Auto Salon. No American coachbuilders were yet familiar with the

New York Auto Salon, 1931: A Waterhouse convertible victoria is at center.

style, of course, and the established companies all required 12 weeks to complete a special design. By the time Packard made its final decision, only seven weeks were left.

The Massachusetts firm of Waterhouse and Company had been started in January 1928 by two Harvard alums, S. Roberts Dunham and Roger Clapp, and two coachbuilders,

Charles Waterhouse and his son, Osborne. In its first year as a builder of custom bodies, the firm received orders for two duPonts and 200 wooden boats. Waterhouse accepted Packard's commission, or dare, of seven weeks to build a car . . . and to copy it from a single, small snapshot of de Sakhnoffsky's convertible victoria.

The job was finished on time. Bob Dunham recalled in a 1961 letter to Osborne's son, Charlie Waterhouse Jr., that they "had not expected to get too much domestic business on this model." However, in a memoir for *The Classic Car,* he related the turn of events upon delivery at New York Packard: "Roger noticed a pair of headlights just behind them as they came to a stop. Two men emerged from this car just behind our convertible victoria and began to examine it with considerable interest. They asked many questions before introducing themselves. One was Alvan Macauley, president of Packard Motor Car Company, and the other was Mr. Lee Eastman, president of New York Packard." The next day,

Owned by M.J. Smith

Macauley placed an order for 10 more 745 convertible victorias, and that led to about 120 in the next three years.

With its newfound prestige, Waterhouse went on to build convertible victoria bodies, and other styles, for Lincoln, Chrysler, Stutz, and Rolls-Royce, among others. It even built the body for an Indy car that had an L-29 Cord driveline. In 1933-34, however, business for coachwork fell sharply, and Waterhouse turned to the furniture business.

In this chapter and the next one, two Packard Series 745 convertible victorias are featured, one by Waterhouse and Company, the American interpreter of the style. It cost $6840 and is supposed to have belonged originally to one of the families connected to the manufacture of Listerine mouthwash. The second 745 convertible victoria is by Proux Carrosserie, a quintessentially French coachbuilder.

The similarities and differences are those of outlook, of course, and of detail, too. The French design is the more coupe-like, distinguished by wider doors, a shorter rear section, and a vertical windshield.

Waterhouse's vision of the model called for a slanted windshield and a sportier stance throughout. The Yanks had altered the de Sakhnoffsky design from the very first, with a roofline that reduced the total height to 5 feet 6 inches, close to a foot lower than the average contemporary car.

The windshield posts blend into the cowl and are even painted to match, while the beltline and body line jog downward behind the doors. The doors are 41-inches wide, requiring heavy-duty hinges and diagonal reinforcements. One Waterhouse addition was an exterior sun visor attached with a piano hinge and trimmed to match the top. The car was typically equipped with auxiliary headlamps and sport mirrors, more bits of business in the overall look.

The Waterhouse convertible victoria overflowed with rakish energy, like the short-lived company that made it.

1930 Deluxe Eight, 745 Proux Convertible Victoria

IN TIMES GONE BY, women who were reared to the exhileration of the hunt took to sports cars and racing, but other women cared less for speed than for style, and for them, the concours d'elegance was created to bring excitement to automobiles.

A concours d'elegance mixed fashion and autos by staging its judging on a car and its coachwork, the woman and her clothing, and occasionally her dog and its fur, or her chauffeur and his uniform. In its heyday between the wars, the concours circuit was continental, with events in Paris, Monte Carlo, Cannes, and Geneva.

To the woman, the day of the concours d'elegance was hers: Mme. Laloy beaming to the crowd from her Rochet-Schneider phaeton at Cannes in June 1931. To the coachbuilders, Guettault frères, it was their day. And to the person who designed Madame's hat, perhaps it was his day.

Maurice Proux was an active member of the concours troupe from 1928 to 1931. He had his own carrosserie in Paris and entered cars in nearly every event. He also served as a juror on occasion. Proux worked on all car styles, from a landaulet for Minerva to a roadster for Alfa Romeo. He also produced bodies for Mercedes-Benz, Hispano-Suiza, Unic, Rolls-Royce, Cord, and Delage. The Proux look was erect and unfrivolous: Even the Alfa roadster had a formal air.

Proux's trademark was the horizontal beltline he utilized. Originally, the enveloping beltline was an innovation of Tom Hibbard, of Hibbard and Darrin, but Proux embraced it, as did many others. Unlike the others, he stayed with it and constantly added refinements. *Auto-Carrosserie*, a French magazine that covered the concours world assiduously, re-

The Proux convertible victoria was discovered in Buenos Aires, in need of attention.

viewed coachbuilders in its issue of November-December, 1931. It acknowledged Proux's dependence on the Hibbard band, while noting, ''There are few changes in the Proux line, which is nonetheless considered a big success.''

Proux resisted the use of overt exterior decoration, in line with most French coachbuilders in 1929-30, preferring in-

stead to simplify lines and highlight small points, like a woman in a plain dress with just one fascinating pin on her collar. For example, he set a medallion of mother-of-pearl into the band on the door of a Delage, a car which took the grand prix at Le Concours d'Elegance Farina-Intran in 1930.

Critiques of the day admired the Proux look, conservative though it was. In 1930, the French coachbuilding magazine, *l'equipment automobile*, made the following assessment: ''Maurice Proux, to all appearances at the top of his profession, has lofty and correct ideas about form.'' While it appears that Maurice Proux would have been content to study form and hone it for 20 more years, others moved more quickly, and exterior plainness gave way. So did Proux Carrosserie, in 1932.

One of the Proux designs for 1930 was a convertible victoria on a Series 745 Packard chassis. Of the history of this car, all that is certain is that it was created in Paris and was found in Argentina in the Sixties. It is said that it was taken

Owned by Mr. & Mrs. Frank R. Miller Jr.

there in 1930 by the French Ambassador to the Argentine, but that cannot be proved.

The convertible victoria was in a sad state of dishevelment when it was imported to America. Yet it was complete and offered a glimpse into the craftmanship of Proux Carrosserie. "It was terrible," recalled Phil Hill of Hill & Vaughn, the Los Angeles firm that restored it. "It was made out of strange bits and pieces, which, of course, custom body people would use if they could. Proux just started with a Packard five-passenger coupe, and there wasn't a single panel that they didn't modify."

The Packard convertible victoria is typical of Proux in its stubborn refusal to rely on distractions to correct problems in form. In silhouette, it would be as strong a design as it is in the light.

1932 Deluxe Eight, 903 Sport Phaeton

IN 1933, JEAN HARLOW was Hollywood's sixth-most popular movie star, according to the *Motion Picture Herald*. She not only earned more than the U.S. President, she earned more than his whole cabinet together. The simple catalyst to the top rank for Harlow was her humor. When Howard Hughes first cast her in a starring role in 1929, he saw her as a siren, nothing more. The producer Irving Thalberg asked her about Hughes at their first interview, when she was being considered for a comedy role at Metro-Goldwyn-Mayer. "Well," Harlow recalled, "one day when he was eating a cookie, he offered me a bite." Thalberg laughed.

"Don't underestimate that," she interjected. "The poor guy's so frightened of germs, it could darn near have been a proposal!"

Into comedy, Jean Harlow soared. Early in 1933, she was cast as a social-climbing hussy in *Dinner At Eight*. The script specified that her accent should be "pure spearmint" and the last scene featured the moment that best captures Harlow's screen personality: "I was reading a book," she remarks to Marie Dressler, who stops dead in her tracks, amazed. "It said that someday machines will replace every profession." "Oh, my dear," Dressler tells her, "that is something you need never worry about."

Thalberg asked Harlow at the interview if she could be comic, if people would laugh at her. "Why not? People have been laughing at me all my life," she said. They may have been laughing at the wrong times before, but *Dinner At Eight* established her as a comedienne of the first order.

During filming of *Dinner At Eight*, Harlow's stepfather was

Miss Jean Harlow, movie star deluxe, liked the top down on her 1932 sport phaeton.

meandering around and took her aside at one point to tell her, "You're a star, sweetheart. You must always act like one." She had him removed from the set.

Even so, in the matter of automobiles, movie stars were encouraged to keep up a certain appearance, if only by competition. In a 1932 edition of *Screen Book*, a fan magazine,

Harlow pointed to her car as an example of her frugality: "It's silly to throw away money . . . I drive a three year-old Cadillac!" On April 15, 1933, she took delivery of a Packard, a 1932 Series 902 Deluxe Eight sport phaeton, at the Thompson Motor Company of Beverly Hills.

The middle of April 1933 was rather late to buy a Ninth Series Packard, since it had been replaced by the company in January. More trenchant for the company and the dealer, it was rather late to sell one. Finding customers for luxury Packard cars was a complicated business in 1931-33. The Great Depression seemed to be settling in for a long run; suicides, to cite a gruesome statistic, were much higher in 1931 than in 1929. Even the families who could afford luxury cars refrained from buying them, for fear of appearing to flaunt their good position.

This, however, was not a concern in Hollywood.

Packard offered 10 body styles on the Series 903 chassis, the shorter, at 142 inches, of the two Deluxe Eight chassis.

Owned by Joyce and Clifford A. Gooding

Thompson Motors still had the sport phaeton on its lot as winter turned to spring. Banks closed in March, Franklin D. Roosevelt took office, and as his 100 Days counted past, Thompson finally unloaded the sport phaeton.

As a new car, it was tan, with dark blue wheels, upholstery, and pinstriping. Optional chrome and glass decorated the car: deluxe windwings on both windshields; dual spotlights; a radiator screen, and fender-mounted rear view mirrors. It was also equipped with free-wheeling, which was supposed to make gear-shifting easier by disengaging the transmission whenever the gas pedal was released. Auburn pioneered the use of free-wheeling on production cars. Though it made the ride smoother and quieter, both dominant Packard attributes, free-wheeling did not catch on with Packard, or with the industry, after the mid-Thirties.

Two other features of Harlow's sport phaeton were standard for the Ninth Series. "Ride Control" allowed the driver—or a fidgety passenger—to adjust the hydraulic pressure of the shock absorbers according to the condition of the road. A similar system was offered by other automakers, including Pierce-Arrow and Franklin.

The "Harmonic Stabilizers" on the front bumper were a homegrown Packard innovation, and they almost seem too

simple for the Twentieth century. Even the name suggests Jules Verne. The Harmonic Stabilizers were weights on either end of the bumper, encased in oil and suspended against springs. They absorbed shocks, not to the wheels individually, but to the frame, from the wheels at odds.

The velveteen ride set a new standard, even among Packards, though the next year Harlow purchased a V-12 Cadillac towncar. She drove her phaeton about 27,000 miles.

"It's the climate that causes me to be so crazy about the outdoors," Harlow told *Screen Book*. "I can't wait to get out in the sun." After her death in 1937, her friend Hunt Stromberg drove the Packard before it was sold in 1939 on a Hollywood used car lot. The couple who bought it then found that the top seemed never to have been put up.

"I love the sun," she said.

1932 Light Eight, 900 Coupe Roadster

G. HENRY STETSON was a maverick kid in 1912, his father being the late hat manufacturer and his mother being, after her remarriage, Sarah Elizabeth Stetson de Queiroz de Sotto Maior Almeida e Vasconcelles, Countess of Eulalia (and of Elkins Park, Philadelphia). The Count of Eulalia, a sculptor by trade, lived in Paris, and with Henry's help, he and the Countess were plotting a revolution to put themselves on the throne of Portugal. The Stetsons sent the Count about $150,000 per year for the cause, but just when he was about to come to Philadelphia to plan the actual battles, the *Titanic* sank, and he decided "not to trust himself to the ocean."

By 1925, Henry was an independent businessman. That year, he tried to start a platinum-mining operation in the Grand Canyon. A federal judge had to explain to him that the Grand Canyon was a national monument.

In 1935, Henry's second wife, Lucretia, who was a socially prominent Philadelphian, divorced him in Los Angeles, charging him with extreme cruelty: He failed to fulfill dinner engagements, drank liquor with the chauffeur, preferred to dine with the servants, and on one occasion, "told a colored serving maid she was the 'best-looking woman at the party.' " Henry didn't contest the divorce, but he did put a barbed wire fence around their house and forbade Lucretia from coming home.

Henry and Lucretia had moved to California in 1928, building a property called "Rancho Sombrero" on 285 acres in

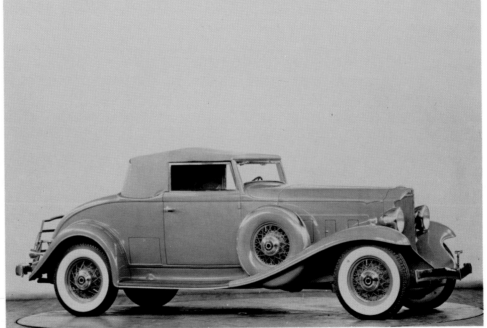

A Packard factory photograph of the Light Eight coupe roadster

the San Fernando Valley. It was probably there that they bought the Light Eight Packard coupe roadster that came out of Henry's estate in the Fifties, according to Jerry Bell Jr., whose father purchased it soon after. As Packard's maverick model of the Thirties, innovative, yet unsuccessful in the market, the Light Eight only appealed to a certain sort.

The Light Eight was a plain attempt to sell cars in a Depression that, by 1931, was clearly not a temporary situation. The niche left by the low-priced Straight Six models of the Twenties beckoned in hard times, and the company tried to fill it with an even smaller, even less-expensive Packard. "It answers the eternal desire for Packard quality, as pronounced today as ever before," the sales catalog bravely asserted, "but repressed for two long years."

The Light Eight engine was basically the same as the Standard Eight, with a nine-bearing crankshaft, and it supplied 110 hp. The lightness throughout gave the model a power-to-weight ratio of one horsepower per 39 pounds, giving it performance that the Standard Eight models did not have. To appeal to a new market segment, one that would not employ a chauffeur, the Light Eight was designed to be easy to drive. A new transmission system, with the vaudevillian name "Packard Silent Synchro-mesh Three-speed," combined with a hand-operated free-wheel-

Owned by Thurman and Dee Decker

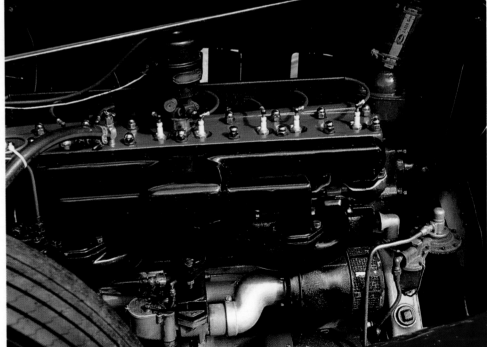

ing unit to allow the driver to bypass the clutch pedal in shifting between second and third. The ''Ride Control'' system of shock-absorber adjustment was standard on the Light Eight, as it was on the rest of the Packard line.

This was Packard's version of a ''people's car.'' It was economical to operate and easy to drive, but people's cars also have to have distinctive looks, and what is more, an ingenuous quality, as if the owner did not need the car nearly as much as the little tike needed an owner. The curved-dash Oldsmobile had it, the Model T, the Austin Seven, the Deux-Chevaux, and, of course, the Volkswagen had it in spades. Packard calculated such a quality into the Light Eight, too. It started with a simplified front end and a grille that sloped forward, like a plow or a steam shovel, from which sprang the Light Eight's street name: ''Shovelnose Packard.''

The factory offered four body styles for the Light Eight: a sedan, a coupe-sedan, a stationary coupe, and the coupe roadster. The coupes had high, rakish doors. Interiors made a virtue of simplicity. Among the features that salesmen were given to tout was a footrest next to the accelerator, hardly a technological breakthrough or a Packard exclusive.

A coupe roadster, like the Stetson car, was priced at $1795, which Packard considered a loss leader. ''Naturally,'' the catalog admonished, ''only a marked public response can continue so featureful a Packard car at so low a price.'' That was correct, and when initial public response ran tepid, prices went up by $100. Finally, with less than 6000 Light Eights sold in the first year-and-a-half, the model was discontinued. Packard had tried to meet the Depression head on, but the Depression won.

Even so, the Light Eight experience would have pleased Henry B. Joy, the former president of Packard. As has been noted, he would say, ''Do something, even if it's wrong.'' With that, Mr. Stetson might concur.

1932 Standard Eight, 902 Seven-Passenger Sedan

I REMEMBER THAT PACKARD WELL. We bought it because it was big enough for the whole family," Ruth Patton Totten recalled of the 1932 Packard seven-passenger sedan that her family used throughout the Thirties. "My father, General Patton, usually bought the newest model of anything going, when he bought a new car. We had Lincolns, Fords, Buicks, et cetera, but we were not an automobile family, being more interested in horses."

George S. Patton Jr. held the rank of major in 1932, when he began three years at Fort Myer, Virginia, as executive officer of the Cavalry. They were three years of brimming days, robust and very social, when peacetime was not wasted on a soldier and his family: foxhunting in the autumn; yachting on the Chesapeake Bay; sometimes watching his wife, Beatrice, and daughters in sailing competitions; playing polo with the War Department team; fencing with masters in New York City; and showing horses throughout the East.

An expert horseman, Patton was an old-school officer of the cavalry, the natural place in the Army for the gentleman-soldier. He clung to tradition, but more deeply than that, he craved glory. "If I knew that I would never be famous," Patton wrote in 1916, "I would settle down and raise horses and have a good time."

Between the wars, a debate raged in the Army concerning the future of the horse in the cavalry, as the armored car seemed poised to replace it—"mechanization," the word itself was a tear in the eye of the old horse soldier.

In fact, Patton had inadvertently commanded the very first motorized military campaign in U.S. history, when he served

George Patton in the Packard with his daughter, Ruth, on her wedding day in 1940

under General John Pershing in the Punitive Expedition of 1916, traipsing throughout Mexican border lands seeking bandits who were marauding in American territory. On May 14, 1916, Patton was sent out with 12 men and three Dodge cars to buy corn. Along the way, he used the cars to infiltrate a bandit-held ranch, jumping with his men from the cars into the fray. Three bandits were killed.

The first sight that Pershing had of the returning force was of the Dodges, the hood of each burdened with the body of a Mexican bandit.

Patton sailed for France in World War I as chief of the Army's Paris motor pool. General Pershing had no personal car to use in Paris, so Beatrice gave him the Pattons' Packard Twin Six. Then George needed a car. "I found another new Packard five seater, one of the last new cars in France," he wrote in a letter home. "So I bought it and then traded it for ours again for myself. I had to pay $4200 for the car on account of the high freight charges." George Patton was a rich man who had married a very rich woman, but certain of his fellow officers still grew ornery about the man in charge of the motor pool being so often seen in a 12-cylinder Packard.

Fifteen years later, with Beatrice, two daughters, and his son with him at Fort Myer, Patton purchased the sedan.

"A New Era," Packard called the year 1932 in advertising,

Owned by Frederick and Carol Mauck

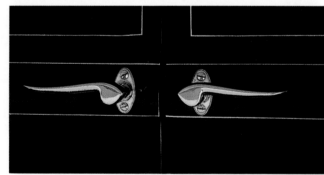

"No longer can anyone say 'I know all about a Packard. We have owned them for years.' " In the Standard Eight, the dominant difference mechanically was in the Ride Control adjustable suspension system and in increased engine insulation. In addition, 1932 was the first year of Packard's Thirties look, effected by the new vee in the grille. That ikon of Packard styling had changed only imperceptably since 1903, but during the Thirties, changes would come far quicker than before, for everyone in search of glory.

1933-34 Twelve, 1108 Dietrich Sport Sedan

PEOPLE WAITED IN LINE two hours to get a good look at the Packard "Car of the Dome" at the Century of Progress in Chicago in 1933. World's fairs being what they are, it would be hard to think of anything of note requiring less of a wait, but it was indeed a crowd-pleaser.

The Car of the Dome was a Packard Twelve, with custom coachwork by Dietrich. Only one was ever made. *The New York Times* breathlessly pondered whether it was a "super deluxe sedan" or "sport-sedan-limousine," but officially, it was a sport sedan, super deluxe nonetheless, with an interior lined with gold-plated appointments; its second nickname was "The Golden Packard."

In the very heart of the Great Depression, the Car of the Dome was priced at $12,000, a tag that would make the real-life custom Packard owner feel poor, let alone the real-life city bus passenger. Yet fairgoers were not waiting in line two hours to resent Packard's Car of the Dome; each was, for a second on sight, its owner.

"A Century of Progress is an abstraction," the Fair president wrote. "It is quite true that whenever Willie Vocalite [the Westinghouse robot] goes into action, he is the center of a fascinated crowd, but there is not one in that crowd who is not infinitely more interesting than Willie Vocalite." The Packard was no symbol of class inequality; it was a draw, like Willie Vocalite or the Thrill House of Crime.

The Car of the Dome was designed by Ray Dietrich, though he was unaware when he drew it that it would be produced as a show car. He was then the source of most of Packard's

Built for the 1933 Century of Progress, the Packard was updated for the '34 Fair.

custom body designs, and the sport sedan was part of a batch that he submitted for the Tenth Series. Dietrich's sport sedan closely resembled his "Individual Custom" designs the previous year, work which broke new ground with its use of slanted vee-windshields and elongated fenders.

On the exterior, a de Sakhnoffsky false hood was inte-

grated to make the front look longer. From there, the hood stretched back uninterrupted to the windshield. Both were touches that gave the car a sleek stance without detracting from its grand presence.

As word reached Packard headquarters that Duesenberg, Pierce-Arrow, and Cadillac were producing special-car showstoppers for the Century of Progress, the sport sedan was selected to represent the Packard-as-Entertainment. It was kept secret, but something about its production could have aroused suspicion. Upon assembly, it was immediately pirated off to an area of the Packard factory reserved for secret projects. Every conceivable interior surface was then gold-plated, from the instrument gauges to the steering column, the gas pedal to the frame on the vanity mirror. It may have been an absurd luxury, but it was becoming to the big Packard. Like other Tenth Series models, it had a wood trim interior worthy of a yacht, in burled Carpathian elm.

The rear compartment was made even more homey by the

Owned by Otis Chandler

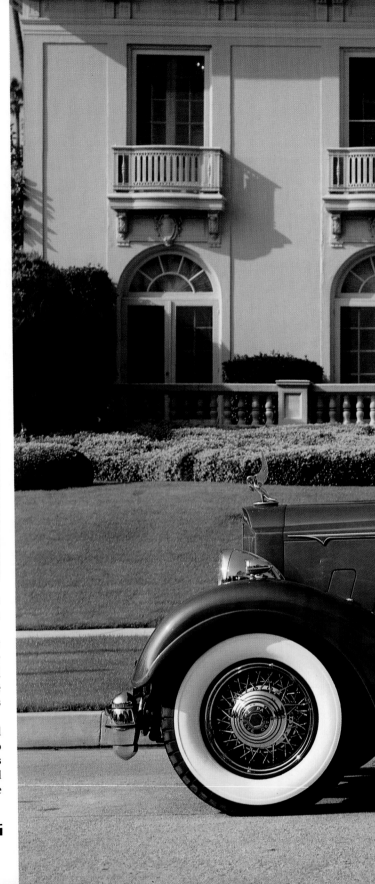

addition of a cellar-ette bar setup built into the division in the back of the front seat. It was appropriate if only as an excuse for more gold-plating, burled wood, and crystal.

While the dream-gentleman in this dream car was busy pouring the horse's necks at the cellar-ette, the dream-lady could be fixing her face at the fold-out dressing table fitted into the right side of the compartment. If, by mistake, she were to sit on the left side, then she—but people in Packards did not make such mistakes.

The Packard arrived in Chicago for the Fair opening and was judged by the committee responsible for such things to be the "highest expression" of the motor car in 1933. It was a safe choice, a true luxury car, not revamped but preened for attention. Anyone who couldn't imagine himself in the back seat of the Golden Packard just wasn't trying.

1934 Twelve, 1108
Dietrich Convertible Sedan

MISS LOUISE BOYD was 32 years old in 1920 when her father died, leaving her $3 million and the family estate in San Rafael, California. He also left her without a relative in the world. She was healthy and active, intelligent and pretty—she could do anything in the world. It may have been momentarily stunning.

So Miss Boyd traveled. In August 1924, she visited Spitsbergen on the coast of Norway as part of a tourist cruise. The view was of frigid cliffs of packed ice, and the other passengers probably responded to it with a draught of hot boullion and a call to the deck porter for more blankets, but Louise Boyd was transfixed. "Cold? Yes, of course," she would say of the Arctic. "But there's unearthly grandeur about it, and I love it."

Two years later, Miss Boyd was ready to outfit and lead her first expedition to the north, to Franz Joseph Land (north of what was then Russia in the Arctic Ocean) to study its geography, plants, and animals. She would sponsor and lead seven more expeditions, and her planning was so meticulous that no injury or crisis ever befell her crews. In fact, in 1928, she was near Norway in a chartered ship, the *Hobby*, when the explorer Roald Amundsen went down in a plane searching for his colleague Umberto Nobile, who had himself gone down in a dirigible. Miss Boyd placed the *Hobby* at the disposal of the international rescue effort and ultimately cov-

Miss Boyd's Packard, on the road in rural Poland, 1934

ered 10,000 miles at sea in the course of the search. Nobile was found, but Amundsen never was. Louise Boyd was honored for her efforts with Norway's Cross of St. Olaf and France's Chevalier of the Legion of Honor, medals that she wore on her gowns at public functions in later years.

"At sea, I don't bother with my hands, except to keep

them from being frozen," she once said. "But I powder my nose before going on deck, no matter how rough the sea is. There is no reason why a woman can't rough it and still be feminine."

Louise Boyd had only a high school education, but her accomplishments soon gained her the respect of the scientific community. "She possessed a freedom that too many of us are afraid to exercise," her minister said of her. In addition to writing two books on the Arctic, Miss Boyd investigated magnetic radio phenomena in Greenland for the National Bureau of Standards during World War II.

In 1934, Louise Boyd was appointed a delegate of the United States government to the International Geographical Congress in Warsaw. At the request of the American Geographical Society, she extended her stay in order to make a photographic study of rural Poland, an effort which resulted in the 1937 book *The Countrysides of Poland*.

In 1935, Poland had 0.7 motor cars per 1000 people; Ger-

Owned by Bill Hirsch

many had 11.9 and Sweden 22.6. In fact, the number of cars in Poland decreased from 1931 to 1936. Roadlife was dominated by pedestrians and ponycarts. Women would commonly walk barefoot and carry their shoes, except through towns. To study the peasantry, however, Louise Boyd opted against assumption of local habit. Instead, she traveled to Poland with her new 12-cylinder Packard convertible sedan, with custom coachwork by Dietrich. She might as well have brought it to King Arthur's Court.

At a cost of $6555, the convertible sedan by Dietrich was one of the most expensive styles offered by Packard on a series 1108 chassis. To make it easier to work in the back, Miss Boyd specified a division window between the front and rear and reading lights for the rear compartment. The vee windshield and the long line of the de Sakhnoffsky false

hood gave the convertible sedan a stately demeanor: It did not become part of the wind; it sliced through it.

Along with the Packard, Miss Boyd brought her chauffeur, Percy R. Cameron, who had been driving her family since 1912. He started out driving a horse and buggy, then graduated to the Boyds' Locomobiles and Miss Boyd's Packards (her last car was a 1951 Packard formal sedan, customized by Ray Dietrich).

From August to October, Louise Boyd, her traveling companion, and Percy Cameron covered 6300 miles throughout Poland. Cars were so scarce that horses shied at the sight of the Packard. People, on the other hand, were drawn to it in droves, proving that Dietrich could be as much a hit in Łódź as in Los Angeles. In the larger cities, garages could be rented overnight. ''My automobile, being a Packard,'' Miss Boyd recounted, ''was frequently found to be too long to permit the [garage] door to be shut.''

At the eminent monastery of Lawra Poczajowska, the monks wore black robes and hats ''like widows' bonnets,'' with veils down the back. In the ancient tradition, they had shoulder-length hair and thick beards. Louise Boyd and her party stayed at the monastery because there were no inns; nor, indeed, was there a garage. The Packard was parked in the churchyard at night, and a monk slept in it, on guard.

Between journeys, Louise Boyd devoted herself to San Rafael and to her home, Maple Lawn, famous for its renowned gardens. She gave big parties and small ones, themselves renowned for her famous Calhoun punch. There are those in San Rafael who are still talking about a certain reception that she gave in honor of Nelson Eddy.

Through a series of financial mistakes, Miss Boyd lost her fortune and Maple Lawn in 1962. Friends from better days provided for her last years in a nursing home. She died in 1972, but no tombstone or memorial to her death stands, just a grand tribute to the life of her: a place in Greenland called ''Miss Louise A. Boyd Land.''

1934 Twelve, 1108 LeBaron Sport Phaeton

PERSONALLY, WE BELIEVE that he is best fitted to be a Packard salesman," the wags at Haverford College wrote when Frederick Hussey graduated in 1932.

Hussey was a lanky, dapper young man at school with a blue-eyed look of determination and a cultivated streak of independence. A science major, he worked his way through every course in the department, often working late into the night in one of the laboratories.

Sophomore year, Hussey bought a new Packard. And Senior year, he bought another: "the most modern and snakiest Packard procurable." Junior year, between Packard purchases, he got married, and all of that made him something of an advertisement on campus for The Good Life.

After college, Hussey scraped together all of his money and bought a 1934 Packard Twelve sport phaeton by LeBaron. "It's a good thing I didn't get so much as a flat tire back then," he later told Packard historian Bob Turnquist, "because I didn't have a dime left over to fix it."

After World War II, Fred Hussey founded the Aeroflex Corporation and owned the Aeroflex-Andover Airport in New Jersey, a showplace that was considered one of the most beautiful, self-contained airports in the country. He kept the Packard at the airport and liked to use it on picnics.

The Eleventh Series 12-cylinder engine develops a high-torque 170 bhp, but the mechanism is so tautly engineered that the ponderous sport phaeton can be slowed to three mph in high gear and then accelerated at will. The vacuum brake system is adjustable from the driver seat, as is the ride

Frederick Hussey, left, at his airport in New Jersey, 1959

control system for the shock absorbers, and the transmission has synchromesh in second and third gears. It may be an intimidating car from the outside, but it is docile from the driver's seat, comparable to the J-12 Hispano-Suiza, among classic cars, in being easy to drive.

The sport phaeton was one of four LeBaron models in the Eleventh Series catalog: a town car and cabriolet made one statement, a conventional one for LeBaron, while a speedster and the sport phaeton had another look, influenced by the Macauley sport coupe.

Edward Macauley was Packard's director of design (and the son of the company president). He was not a designer himself but had two attributes (other than being the son of the company president): He was representative of the typical Packard customer, and he knew what he liked when he saw it. After a trip to Europe in 1933, Macauley had a sport coupe created at Packard to reflect his newly acquired Continental tastes. The result was organic but slick, with a gently recumbent rear profile, pontoon fenders, and a de Sakhnoffsky false hood. A handful of sales were racked up for the sport coupe—a surprising and pleasing Packard, even to its arrowhead-shaped rear quarter windows.

LeBaron Inc. was in no position in 1933-34 to resist directives from Packard's director of design, and so it interpreted

Owned by Bob Bahre

Opposite page, front to back: 1934 sport phaeton by LeBaron, 1934 sport coupe by Packard, 1934 speedster by LeBaron.

the sport phaeton and speedster as derivitives of the Macauley sport coupe. The speedster, on the 134⅞-inch chassis, was an explosive, active design. The sport phaeton, on a chassis one foot longer, is more of a single shape, though the fenders, running boards, and headlamps are still distinct. Like the sport coupe, it has a vee-windshield. A consistent design throughout, the sport phaeton is a peak in the transition from the erect architecture of earlier cars to the rather bulbous aerodynamics to come.

LeBaron stayed in business until the war, refining its suave look on the Chrysler Thunderbolt and Newport show cars of 1940. When Chrysler acquired LeBaron's parent company, Briggs Body, in 1953, it was quite a blow to Packard, which had grown dependent on Briggs. Less important to Packard was that all future LeBaron cars would be Chryslers.

In the same year, 1953, a '34 LeBaron sport phaeton was displayed at the International Motor Sports Show in New York, an indication to Hussey that his car was becoming a serious asset. "Once somebody told him how valuable it was, he built a climate-controlled room for it," his son Derrick said. It was exercised at speeds of over 100 mph on a 2000-foot runway at the Aeroflex-Andover Airport.

Beginning in 1957, Hussey had one of his employees take the sport phaeton to Classic Car Club of America car shows. It usually made an appearance at the annual January meet in Buck Hill Falls, Pennsylvania, where cars and owners congregated on snow-covered roads. In 1960, Hussey drove the Packard himself to Buck Hill Falls, and that year it was the overall winner with a score of 100 points, only the third car in club history to merit a perfect score.

In Hussey's eyes, though, the sport phaeton probably never looked any better or worse than it did the day he bought it. Only after his death in 1977 was it auctioned off, still in original condition.

1937 Six, 115-C Convertible Coupe

I T WAS 1937 when I first saw my 115-C convertible coupe. I was a boy of about nine years-old," Wallace Walmsley said. "It was owned by Joleen Nevitt, an attractive blond girl of 18. The car was purchased by her parents as a high school graduation gift, picked up on May 3rd, 1937, at Jordan Packard in San Diego.

"We lived up on a hill in Mission Hills in San Diego, on Brant Street at Curlow Circle. The Nevitts lived below us on Reynard Way. From my bedroom on the third floor, I looked out my window on the Nevitts' driveway, which curled around to a courtyard in the back. The 115-C was yellow in those days, and I could see it coming and going, when Joleen wasn't away at college. She went to Stanford University. Mr. Nevitt was vice-president of a bank in San Diego, and he invested in real estate on the side. They had several Packards over the next few years. I remember a 1936 chauffeur-driven limousine, painted dark blue, and a grey 1936 One Twenty business coupe, used by Joleen's grandmother. We were a Packard family, too. My dad owned Packards and Pierce-Arrows, but when Pierce-Arrow closed down, he bought Packards exclusively for the rest of his life. He retired from business in the Twenties, when the Japanese and Chinese confiscated his tea and coffee holdings overseas. After that, he took up in real estate and horse racing.

"Back to my 1937 115-C Packard: I kept seeing it until World War II broke out, at which time we moved to New York state. Many families were moving east, as there was a scare that the Japanese might land in California. At the end of the war, we moved back. After two years of college, I got

A business day at Jordan Packard in San Diego, at the time the 115-C was introduced

married. My wife and I were driving down El Cajon Boulevard in San Diego, and I spotted Joleen's 115-C Packard at a Chrysler dealership. She and her husband had traded it in on a 1950 Chrysler the day before. It looked and drove like a new car, with 32,000 miles on the odometer."

Walmsley bought the car for $185.

For Packard, the 115-C was like a junior version of its famous Junior car, the One Twenty. It had the same chassis design and much the same styling, but it was shorter and offered Packard's first six-cylinder engine since 1928.

The 115-C Six was named for its 115-inch wheelbase, five inches shorter than that of the One Twenty. The next model year, 1938, the wheelbase was extended to 122 inches. In terms of displacement, the 115-C Six, at 237 cid, was the smallest Packard engine since the 1901 Model C, at 183.8 cid, but the 100 bhp that it produced was adequate for its dimensions and light weight.

Many people seemed to think so, taking into account that at a base price of $795, it was the least expensive car that Packard had ever produced. In 1937, when it was introduced, it accounted for 64,401 sales, boosting overall Packard deliveries to a record 122,593. Sales in subsequent years were uneven, but the One Twenty and the One Ten (as the 115-C Six was later renamed) succeeded in insulating the com-

Owned by Wallace Walmsley

pany from the failing fortunes of its luxury line.

The Packard Straight Six models of 1921 to 1928 were lower in performance than the company's eight-cylinder models but lacked little in the way of luxury. With the 115-C Six, even more than the One Twenty, Packard was searching out a new market.

Not only did the 115-C rob sales from the likes of Hudson, Plymouth, Nash, and Oldsmobile, it satisfied loyal Packard customers who, like the Nevitts, did not require the same level of luxury in every car they bought.

The Nevitts, however, certainly tried to compensate. The base convertible coupe sold for $910, but their car had cost $1147, its option list reading approximately like the index page of the Packard Accessory Book: trunk rack, radio, heater, defroster and deflector, visors, outside mirror with Packard script, locking gas cap, goddess of speed hood ornament, banjo steering wheel, cat's eye cigar lighter, center bumper guard, and a radio speaker for the rumble seat.

"It's solid and soft and quiet," Walmsley said, having driven it 144,000 miles himself throughout California. "At 65 mph, with the windows and the top up, it's very quiet and insulated from road vibration."

A Packard through and through, as the company claimed, the 115-C was the dreamer's Packard for those who couldn't remotely afford a Twelve. In just one year, more people owned up to that piece of the dream than had ever actually bought a 12-cylinder Packard.

1937 Super Eight, 1501 Five-Passenger Coupe

"M Y DREAM," she once said, "is to provide a place where the sons and daughters of factory workers can go to college."

Julia Thompson was the only child of Major Albert Brooker, a Civil War hero from Torrington, Connecticut. After the war, the Major amassed a tidy fortune, consisting of land, securities, and a brass factory, yet he was "a man of simple tastes, exceedingly democratic in his habits." His daughter idolized him. She graduated from Miss Porter's School for Girls in Farmington in 1900, and a few months later, she married Austin Thompson, a young dentist in Torrington.

The Thompsons seemed to follow the Major's example, living quietly in his Victorian house on Albert Street in Torrington, with an occasional trip to Florida to visit relatives. When they were newlyweds, they drove a Stevens-Duryea tourer, a proper New England choice. In about 1916, they bought a coupe which served them for nearly 20 years, and they grew very fond of it; Julia even had herself photographed with it on the sands of Daytona Beach, Florida.

In 1937, eight years after Dr. Thompson retired from practice, the couple picked out a new car, a Packard Super Eight five-passenger coupe, painted black. A chauffeur-driven coupe is hardly evidence of life in the grand style for someone who could afford anything he wanted, yet a long-time resident of Torrington can still recall the sight of Dr. Thomp-

Mrs. Julia Thompson at Daytona Beach with her much-beloved coupe, circa 1916

son in the front of the Super Eight Packard, being driven around town by his chauffeur.

The Super Eight model was in the midst of a change of identity in 1937. The Packard Motor Car Company combined the standard Eight and Super Eight models under the name "Super Eight," though utilizing the standard Eight engine.

After this sleight of hand, the output of the so-designated Super Eight dropped from 150 bhp at 3200 rpm in 1936 to 135 bhp in 1937. The car was still capable of 80 mph, however, and it featured chassis improvements over the 1936 model in hydraulic brakes and independent front suspension. Most importantly, Packard was able to drop the base price of a Super Eight from $2990 to $2335, even while retaining the styling and appointments of the 1936 Super Eight. The consolidation of Packard's Senior Eights simplified production lines at the factory and distinctly separated them from the low-priced One Twenty.

The move also reflected Packard's retrenching in the face of a growing shadow of competition from Cadillac, which had, in 1936, passed Packard in fine-car sales. A war with General Motors was waged on a kaleidoscope of fronts, and in the middle Thirties, Packard was surrounded by them, turning from one to another, one to another. While Packard had great success with its One Twenty in the mid-Thirties

Owned by Mrs. Gloria Malumphy

and Packard Twelves generally outsold Cadillac's 12 and 16-cylinder models, in the middle, Cadillac offered a new V-8 engine in snappy styles that hooked many former Packard customers.

The Super Eight coupe, at once opulent and humble, did not sell well in 1937, and today, only three examples are known to exist. It is such an unassuming car to be one of the rarest Packards of the Thirties, yet it reflected the peculiar psychology of customers like the Thompsons: a very low level of flash in a fairly high level of wealth.

The Thompsons' Super Eight Packard was still in occasional use 23 years after it was purchased, still in the Albert Street garage. Few changes had been made through the years

to the Major's house, a pile of ideas in 19th century architecture: turrets, verandahs, arched windows, gables, and gingerbread, of course.

The day after Thanksgiving in 1960, a lawyer was called to the house. Mrs. Thompson was then 84 years old, a childless widow ravaged by a heart condition and chronic arthritis. Dr. Thompson had died in 1954, and two years later, two of Torrington's strongest law firms, already eyeing the Thompson fortune for charities mentioned in various Thompson wills, brought the question of Mrs. Thompson's competency into court. She was judged to be capable. In her last years, her house bustled with servants, each of whom she insisted upon paying herself, in cash.

The lawyer who was called to the house had drafted a will for Mrs. Thompson one year before, but he was so rushed by her desire to sign it on the holiday weekend that he had to bring his wife and daughter to serve as witnesses. One of the servants led them through the house to see Mrs. Thompson, who was attended by a nurse. She could muster only a shaky ''X'' in lieu of a signature.

Six days later, she died, leaving her estate to the creation of a campus for the University of Connecticut at Torrington.

1938 Twelve, 1608
Rollston Dual-Cowl Phaeton

King Feisal II at the age of four, riding his first pony

WHEN PRINCE GHAZI of Iraq was sent to school at Harrow in 1925, he struggled with the English language but embraced the sporting automobile with the speed of summer lightning. Because he was too young to drive on public roads, Iraqi officials arranged for the private use of Brooklands racetrack, where the prince would drive around and around, alone.

"An enthusiastic motorist, he liked to drive his own car as often as possible," *The Iraq Times* reported in 1939, when Ghazi was 27 and the crowned king of Iraq. He owned a supercharged Auburn speedster and a Mercedes-Benz cabriolet with a phosphorescent paint scheme, in addition to a plane that he piloted himself. Ghazi liked to drive the Mercedes across the countryside at night, speeding through the black velvet air in his glow-in-the-dark car. "The natives consider it an apparition," an American visitor told *The New York Times* in 1937, "and it both frightens and pleases them."

In 1938, the royal family gave Ghazi's son, Feisal II, a Packard Twelve dual-cowl phaeton by Rollston. The car was probably a reflection of the father's taste, and it was certainly at his disposal: Feisal was just a three-year-old.

In regal maroon, with flags forward and a tricolor on the front bumper, the Packard made a stately parade car. The Sixteenth Series 12-cylinder chassis was in its second-last year of production, a perfected machine that delivered a silky 175 bhp. Even on the longest wheelbase available, 139⅜ inches, and with a heavy Rollston body, the phaeton moves without noticeable effort.

Packard had built its last phaeton in 1936, and so the Iraqi car had to be custom-bodied. The choice in coachbuilders was slim in 1937, but one of the best, the Rollston Company, was still operating in New York, finishing one car about every two weeks—a trickle compared to the firm's fat days in the Twenties.

Feisal's phaeton was built in the fall of 1937, just months before Rollston went into receivership in April 1938. The core of the company returned in the autumn, as "Rollson," and as such, it built 50 bodies before the outbreak of World War II. "Those last years proved one thing," wrote Rollston/Rollson designer Rudy Creteur in *The Classic Car*, "that custom bodies were finished. Only Packard made a suitable chassis to receive such bodies and their sales were limited."

No coachbuilder built a sturdier car than did Rollston. All metalwork was hammered in the shops, not salvaged from other car bodies; wood frames were thick and lasting, reinforced with brass supports. "Everything at Rollston was done to create the strongest body," Creteur wrote. The phaeton is bulky, but its long lines make it graceful.

In 1938, when the young prince took possession of his

Owned by Robert L. Meyer

Packard, Iraq was a country blessed with abundant water and oil but warped by a feudal economy. In the last week of March 1939, four-year-old Feisal was a ribbon-winner at the Royal Baghdad Horse Show, a tiny, serious figure riding his pony around the ring, enveloped by applause from the crowd. Just before midnight on April 5, King Ghazi was out driving, apparently in his phosphorescent Mercedes, when he was killed in an accident.

Feisal was king. He had his Packard and a fortune beyond it; he had his mild manner; and he had a regent and an uncle who disenfranchised common Iraqis more thoroughly than had Ghazi on his worst day. To commemorate the end of World War II, Feisal paraded through Baghdad in the back of the Packard, waving and smiling. According to his cousin, King Hussein of Jordan, ''Feisal never harmed anybody and never had enough control of events to make a single major political decision that could have angered anybody.''

At 5 a.m. on July 14, 1958, army revolutionaries stormed into the Royal Palace, where Feisal and his family were sleeping. The regent and Feisal's uncle were slain immediately. The officers were going to spare the innocent Feisal, but as an after-thought, he was killed, too.

Carried to adulthood in vehicles as Western and as steady as cars like the Packard Twelve, a limited young man might be forgiven for losing touch with Arab culture in its very purest form—forgiven by history, at any rate.

1940 One Twenty, 1801 Station Sedan

SEBASTIAN S. KRESGE, the dime-store king, was given to proclamations, and because he was a king, people took note:

"When one begins at the bottom and learns to scrape, everything comes easy."

"I never spent more than thirty cents for lunch in my life."

"I was successful because I saved and I heeded good advice."

Partly because he never spent more than thirty cents on lunch, S.S. Kresge was in a position to donate $65 million to charity from 1924 to 1966. He started out as a tinware salesman; 18-hour days and early advice from the likes of F.W. Woolworth and J.G. McCrory led to a chain of five-and-dime stores that later led to the K Mart Corporation.

Kresge was so parsimonious that he put paper in his shoes when the soles wore out and gave up golf because he felt he couldn't afford to lose golf balls off the fairway. Being such an inveterate bargain-hunter, he had genuine respect for the customers of his stores.

Yet, according to *The New York Times*, one pleasure that Kresge indulged—in his own way—was motoring: "His first car was an air-cooled Franklin which, according to an associate, 'he ran until the wheels fell off.' In the 20's, he drove a Packard to the limit of its life expectancy; in later years, he also picked his automobiles for their durability rather than their chrome."

In 1940, running true to form, Kresge bought a One Twenty station sedan. The One Twenty was the workhorse of the Packard sales line-up; from 1935 until 1940, it eclipsed all other Packard models except its own little brother, the six-

S.S. Kresge at age 90, feeding the pet deer he raised from a fawn

cylinder One Ten. The One Twenty was a sparely constructed eight-cylinder car. As Packard's luxury line lost ground to Cadillac in the mid-Thirties, and both lost ground to changing times, Packard opened up a new market—or theater of war—in producing the Olds-beater, the One Twenty. It may have compromised the prestige of the name Packard," but it also kept it alive and prosperous.

Originally, the One Twenty was named for its wheelbase, 120 inches. Its in-line eight-cylinder engine produced 110 bhp, and it had a top speed of about 85 mph. By 1940, the wheelbase was changed to 127 inches, but that year, the horsepower was rated at 120, which was certainly fitting.

Packard had flirted with the station wagon style on its junior cars in the middle of 1937, but production was crowded enough during that boom year, and the style was dropped. It was resurrected in 1940, when Packard had greater need to cater to market niches.

Before the war, station wagons were a symbol of the country life. They were rugged and inexpensive, but nonetheless, they suggested relaxed wealth the way that Wellington boots and a thorn-proof coat suggest the same in England. "When I was a little girl in the late Thirties," a former Bronx resident recalled, "a limousine or a sports car would go by, and we would all gawk at it, of course. But

Owned by Kenneth C. Gibson

those cars were in the stratosphere as far as we were concerned. A station wagon would go by, and I'd get a pang, sure that it was going to a pretty house in Connecticut or Bucks County—with a fire in the fireplace.''

The leader in the station wagon field was by far the Ford Motor Company. In fact, Ford had offered the first factory-built station wagon in 1922. Performance, of course, was never a standard by which a station wagon was judged, and Plymouth was the second-most popular make. Packard did not even enter the market until it began to offer the more modest One Twenty and One Ten chassis.

In the Fifties, station wagons lost their panache and became the most middle-class of conveyances. One indication of this is the use of metal bodywork. When Kresge bought his Packard station sedan, ''woodies'' were made of wood: mahogany and ash, with oak trim in the interior. The company recommended that the paneling be sanded and freshly varnished once a year. This was a job for a servant, not for a busy housewife.

S.S. Kresge bought his One Twenty station sedan to use on his 26-acre farm in Mountainhome, Pennsylvania, in the Pocono Mountains, not far from his birthplace. In the early Thirties, he went to inspect the property and fell in love with the owner, Mrs. Clara Swaine, who later became his third wife. Kresge's very first business venture, at the age of eight in 1875, was in selling honey from his own beehives. On the farm in Mountainhome, he resumed this enterprise, and even in his nineties, he was still using his Packard to haul jars of honey into town to sell at market. He also sold apples that were grown in his orchard. Primarily, though, the car was used as it was intended literally, not to ferry runny-nosed skiers to the slopes, but to meet visitors at the train station.

S.S. Kresge died in 1966 at the age of 99. Clara Kresge sold

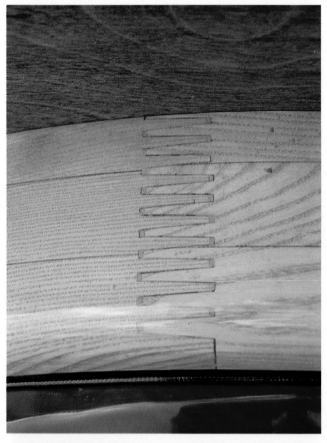

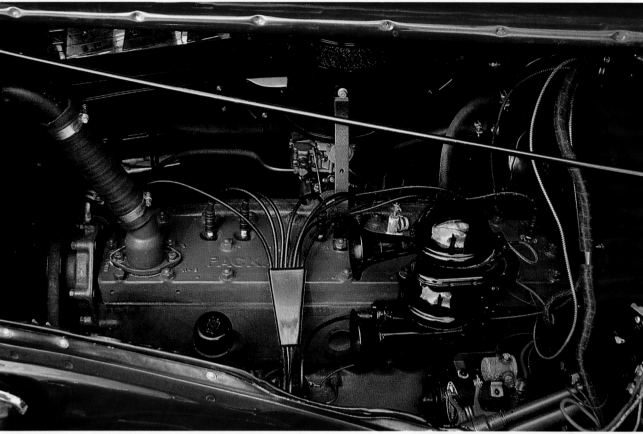

the station sedan in 1974. At that time, it had 57,000 miles on the odometer. The only other car in the five-car garage was a 1954 Cadillac limousine.

In 1953, S.S. donated the funds for Kresge Hall at Harvard University's School of Business. At the dedication ceremony, he was asked to speak. He approached the lectern and advised the students, "I never made a dime talking." That was his whole speech. In the Fifties, when Kresge's five-and-dime stores evolved into the K Mart empire, S.S. oversaw the change, and he didn't retire as chairman of the board until 1966 when he was 98 years old.

In 1957, the directors of the Kresge Company were invited to Mountainhome for S.S. Kresge's 90th birthday party. S.S. took them on a tour of the farm, introduced them to his pet deer, which he had raised as an orphaned fawn, and blew out all the candles on the cake. His son recalled, "He greeted us jovially—and with a characteristic quip reflecting his thrift, he invited us all to stay for the rest of the month!"

S.S. was born on July 31.

1940 Custom Super-8, 1807 Darrin Sport Sedan

NOT A CAR for those whose visions are cast in the staid, conventional mold,'' said the advertisement in the December 1939 issue of *Fortune* magazine; the subject was a Packard sport sedan by Darrin.

Packard's custom cars satisfied extremes in 1940. For customers who were cast in that staid mold, Packard offered a town car and cabriolet by Rollson. For the ''adventurous, the daring, the unfettered and free,'' it offered Darrin.

Dutch Darrin was an American of lifelong youth, who made Paris his home after World War I. With his partner, Tom Hibbard, he developed a reputation in coachbuilding there, a reputation that did not suffer when Hibbard left the firm in 1931. In fact, when Hibbard left, people were forced to recognize that Dutch Darrin, salesman extraordinaire, was an exciting designer in his own right.

By 1936, however, business was slow in Paris, and Darrin took his leave on a German freighter bound for New York. He could even make retreat a glamourous affair, including with his personal effects on board ship a deHaviland Puss Moth airplane, which he flew from New York to Los Angeles. Los Angeles—more specifically, Hollywood—succumbed to both his charms and his talents. As debut custom cars on the West Coast, Darrin made a convertible victoria on a 1937 Ford V-8 chassis and a roadster on a '37 Packard One Twenty chassis. They continued the direction he had followed in Paris: longer hood, lower profile, cutaway doors, and slop-

A detail from the ad in *Fortune*, 1939: bringing Darrin to the nation

ing tail section. In all of these ways, the designs contrasted with America's production cars, not so much in direction but in degree. Darrin had an impatience that the big companies did not have, and he used it to his advantage.

The Darrin look was a sensation, as it would have been anywhere in America, but Hollywood had a peculiar appetite

for sensation, and Darrin rode a crest of publicity because of it. He soon convinced Packard to sell his convertible victorias through dealerships and to promote them nationally, in magazines such as *Fortune*. One Darrin-Packard left the L.A. shop every two weeks; about 24 were completed before demand forced Darrin to move production to the old Auburn factory in Connersville, Indiana, in 1939.

Darrin's first closed Packard (since leaving Paris) was a sport sedan on a 1939 Custom Super-8 chassis. This prototype represented an important step for Darrin. If he was to progress beyond a Hollywood toymaker, a closed car was a necessity. However, the prototype was expensive and complicated to build. It was priced at $6100 in 1940, when a Darrin convertible victoria cost $4593 (his convertible sedan, also introduced in 1940, was $6332).

Still, the market for a sport sedan seemed promising, so Darrin tried to simplify production by using the bottom portion of a factory One-Eighty sedan, lowered, of course, with

Owned by Eugene Tareshawty

a lengthened hood and the cast vee-windshield developed at the Los Angeles shop. Darrin sculpted a new roof, while running boards—anathema to him—were optional. The first Connersville sport sedan, featured in these pages, was built for the Ames family of Easton, Massachusetts, who used it as a limousine. Probably only one other sport sedan was made, for a total of three. Overall, less than 200 Darrin-Packards were built from 1937 to 1941.

Rudy Stoessel was Darrin's production manager in the Los Angeles shop during 1938. He recalled that Darrin was a dreamer and an artist, emphatic about his ideas, but rather distracted as a businessman. He liked to play polo; he liked to go to parties; he liked to fly his airplane and sail. The Darrin-Packard made a terrific impact on the automobile world, but as a business, it lost money. Not even success could keep up with Dutch Darrin.

1940 Packards by Darrin. Left to right: convertible victoria, sport sedan, convertible sedan.

1941 Custom Super-8, 1907 Formal Sedan

JOHN SARGENT PILLSBURY was out driving his Packard one day in 1908: a 30-year-old man at the controls in his family's own town of Minneapolis. Except that the car broke down on the side of the road, and the scion of the Pillsbury-Washburn Mills had to get out and get under.

While Pillsbury was fixing the car, a family friend named Mr. Pennington happened by in his horse and buggy, with his stepdaughter. Mr. Pennington offered to help, but Pillsbury declined. So Mr. Pennington introduced him to his stepdaughter, Juty Lawler. In 1911, Pillsbury married Miss Lawler. Obviously, he forgave the Packard for breaking down: Forty years later, he still owned a Packard car. Fifty years later, he was still married to the former Miss Lawler.

The Pillsburys had six children, and the family spent part of the year at their second home in Palm Beach, Florida. In April 1941, Pillsbury attended the West Palm Beach Auto Show and purchased a Custom Super-8 One-Eighty formal sedan off the floor.

The car was black when it was new, one of about 100 1941 formal sedans sold on Packard's One-Eighty chassis. The same chauffeur drove the car throughout the 17 years that Pillsbury owned it, often on the trip between Minnesota and Florida. According to the current owner, Jerry Peterson, the only sound at 60 mph is the ticking of the clock.

With the discontinuation of Packard Twelve production in 1939, the One-Eighty assumed the mantle of Packard's most prestigious model. The Super-8 engine supplied 160 bhp, comparable to the Twelve's 175 bhp, but the One-Eighty didn't stand alone as the Twelve had; it leaned heavily on

Wedding Day, January 4, 1947: George and Sally Pillsbury in the family Packard

its little brothers and sisters, in engineering and styling.

Straddling the good old days and the brave new world, the One-Eighty was identical mechanically to the less exalted One-Sixty model. Both came on wheelbases of 127, 138 (as on the Pillsbury car), or 144 inches. To manufacture the image of luxury required of the One-Eighty, it was ostensibly

built to order, by either Packard or one of three designated coachbuilders.

Even locating three going coachbuilders was an accomplishment in 1940-42; they were Rollson, Darrin, and LeBaron. Packard's own offerings were not as distinctive as the others, looking suspiciously akin to the One Twenty, but in quality, they were well up to the standard established by the prewar coachbuilding companies.

Wood abounded in Pillsbury's car, in the window molding, inlayed with walnut burl and silver trim, and in the two vanities, appointed with beveled mirrors, perfume bottles, leather notebooks, and sterling silver pencils. By buying the car at the Auto Show, Pillsbury forfeited his choice of options on the car and accepted it as it was, with an electric divider window between the front and rear compartments, electric side windows, a smaller rear window than standard with blind rear quarters, mohair carpeting, and a storage compartment fitted with a Jaegar clock, among other features.

Owned by Jerry Peterson

In the Pillsbury family, cars usually wore out before they were sold. Yet in the Fifties, the formal sedan still made the trip back and forth to Florida, carrying not the family, but the servants. The Packard was finally sold in 1958, with 100,275 miles on the odometer, traded in for a new Cadillac. Martin Peterson bought it a few weeks later, and his son, Jerry, restored it in the early Eighties. In August 1987, the car and its owners were guests at a Pillsbury family reunion, in honor of Mrs. Juty Pillsbury's 100th birthday. John Pillsbury had died in 1968, in Florida.

Pillsbury was a tall, lanky man, a dapper dresser who favored pin-stripe suits. In his lapel, he always wore a red carnation. ''What I like best is knowing people,'' he said when he retired from his company. ''I've always loved life and it has been good to me.''

He had wanted to be a diplomat when he was a student

at the University of Minnesota, and he intended to go to Paris for further study, after graduation in 1900, but in his senior year, his father and great-uncle—founders of the Mills—both died. John Pillsbury had to stay home to manage the business with his twin brother, Charles, and his cousin, Alfred, commonly referred to as ''the football hero son of the governor'' (which he was). After four years, John was sent abroad to the Orient, on the pretext of company business, in what he later called ''his foreign correspondent years.'' When he came home, it was for good.

In his eighties, John Pillsbury still worked every day at his rolltop desk at Pillsbury headquarters. One of his few hobbies was his devotion to University of Minnesota football. On game days, he liked to drive his grandchildren into town for lunch at the Minneapolis Athletic Club, then over to Gopher Stadium for the game. That is how one of them remembers the formal sedan and John Pillsbury.

1941 Custom Super-8, 1907 Custom Convertible Victoria

EXCITING IDEAS on automobile styling soared out of Southern California just before World War II, fed by the convergence of ready money, an undemanding climate, Mr. Dutch Darrin, and the show-off spirit of Hollywood. The new look featured a lowered profile and cutaway doors, but more important, it took the scientific taint out of aerodynamics and replaced it with a spicy cologne.

Darrin, of course, started the revolution with his daring convertible victorias, developed in 1937-38. Celebrities and people who wanted to look like celebrities quickly filled up Darrin's order books, leading to a national Darrin-Packard line in 1939-41 (featured in an earlier chapter of this book). However, the same insouciant personality that gave such freshness to Darrin's designs also affected the production of his early cars. For example, on a Darrin-Packard made in 1938, the metalwork under the fenders was simply left the way it had been cut: unrolled, untucked, and unfinished. Darrin's Packards were breathtaking to look at, but they had the reputation of being rattle-boxes that were just as breathtaking to ride in.

Just across the mountains from Darrin's Hollywood shop, the Pasadena firm of Bohman & Schwartz reigned as Southern California's finest custom coachbuilder. Organized out of the remnants of the Walter Murphy Company, Bohman & Schwartz never built a line of cars or slipped into one particular specialty. Rather, it made a business of the one-off body. A typical job was in the reconstruction of a 1939 Packard Twelve sedan (pictured on page 175). Bohman &

The original rendering of the convertible victoria, made by W. Everett Miller

Schwartz lowered the body by five inches, re-drew the rear window, and incorporated such amenities as extra cigar lighters and the concealment of the radio antenna in one of the running boards.

When the Darrin convertible victoria made a hit in Los Angeles in 1938, customers naturally approached Bohman &

Schwartz for a sturdy, Pasadena-version of the new look. ''My father built a LaSalle convertible, very much like a Darrin job,'' Chris Bohman recalled. That was sold to Pete Burroughs of the adding-machine company. Then he did two Cadillac coupes and converted them the same way, with the drop doors and the chrome vee-windshield.

''A man named Williams, from the family that made Williams shaving creams, came to us next,'' Bohman continued. ''He wanted the same type of convertible victoria, but on a 148-inch wheelbase, Packard One-Sixty chassis. He wanted us to do just what Darrin was doing and what we had done on the Cadillacs.''

That was in June of 1940. ''Soon after,'' Bohman said, ''a Packard dealer from Beverly Hills got in touch with Bohman & Schwartz and asked if we would go ahead and build some more, but on the One-Eighty Packards and on the middle wheelbase, at 138 inches. We built three.''

Designed, or at least interpreted, by Everett Miller, the

Owned by Murray MacLeod Gammon

convertible victorias were genuine refinements of Darrin's originals. The front fenders fed back into the doors, which necessarily opened from the back, not from the front like Darrin-Packards. Darrin tried to reduce chrome decorations, but Bohman & Schwartz added two per side. One is positioned along the base between the front and rear fenders. It indicates a running board, but is not one, of course. The second chrome strip is the focal point of the car, running back from the corner of Packard radiator shell three-quarters the length of the car. It is a falling arc that signs the piece for Bohman & Schwartz.

Coachbuilding and the whole classic-car era was drawing to a close when Dutch Darrin and Bohman & Schwartz produced their spirited convertible victorias of 1938-41. As cars, they were flamboyant and completely self-indulgent, a trip to Hollywood that just might have lasted if not for the war.

Packards by Bohman & Schwartz. Left, 1939 Twelve club sedan; right, 1941 Super-8 convertible victoria

1941 Clipper Eight, 1951 Touring Sedan

THE 1941 CLIPPER was an all-new look from a company that had grown big on small changes in styling. It was low; it was wide; the front fenders were sculpted into the hood; the running boards were vestigial; the head lamps were integral; and the lines overall were simplified or erased. Yet it still had the aura of a Packard. Looking back on the interruption caused by World War Two, the Clipper was not the last of the prewar cars; it was the first of the postwar cars.

The Clipper used the 282 cid in-line eight engine that had passed muster in 185,000 One Twenty Packards since 1935. The chassis was all-new, though, to allow the car to sit lower than previous Packards. While the interior may have dented the insouciance—and the haberdashery—of men in top hats, it was actually more spacious than any other Packard in the 1941 line-up.

The design of the Clipper emanated largely from the vision of Dutch Darrin, a designer of international reputation who usually managed to stay out of step—as an artist will. As an independent contractor, he supplied the first draft of the Clipper idea, giving the big car a rhythmic flow with the grand sweep of the front fenders back into the doors (in Darrin's original design, they went all the way back to the rear fenders, like a gigantic sports car).

During the spring and summer of 1941, excitement surrounded the new model, and dealers resorted to waiting lists as demand exceeded production capacity. The Clipper hit the middle mark as a car built to luxury standards but relaxed

Frank Mellon in Meriden, Connecticut, with his 1941 Clipper

for everyday use: a decidedly postwar vision of a luxury car.

Frank Mellon, a postman in Meriden, Connecticut, wanted one. Not simply because it was the hot new Packard to have if you were a Packard man, which he was, three times proven, but also because it had wide doors and accommodating seats. Mellon took care of his ailing aunt, whom he

had to lift in and out of his car. The configuration of the Clipper made it easier on them both.

Jack Scanlon was a portly, bespectacled man, and he was the postmaster of Meriden. He further busied himself as the owner of Scanlon Packard downtown. When a Meriden postman wanted a Packard, financing was at least a civilized affair, since the dealer and the postman's boss were so well-acquainted. Scanlon encouraged his men with a five-percent discount on new Packards, which was impressive, considering that he made employees at the dealership pay full price.

The showroom at Scanlon Packard showed but one car. To see the other three, customers had to walk in the back to the service bay. "We sold the six- and eight-cylinder models, mostly," recalls the firm's service manager, Larry Miller. "Over in Middletown, they went in for 12-cylinder Packards."

Mellon ordered a black Clipper at a total price of $1459.26—entitling him to a Meriden-Postman's Discount of $76.25.

Owned by Rick and Susan Reale

The arithmatic calculations were jotted on the cover of a sales brochure; additions of a radio, heater, deluxe hood ornament, and Packard running lights made the total $1546.85.

The first Clipper to arrive at Scanlon Packard was maroon. Mellon wouldn't accept it, however anxious he was, and on May 23, his black Clipper was delivered. In all, about 10 Clippers were sold in Meriden in 1941-42.

It was a well-balanced car, quiet and easy to steer, shift, and control. Mellon took fastidious care of his car, waxing it just about as often as he drove it. In 1947, he was out for a ride when he saw Jack Scanlon ahead, in a new Packard. By way of a Yankee sort of a greeting, he passed him.

Scanlon found his way to the Mellon residence and laid two one-thousand-dollar bills on the table. ''Frank,'' he said,

"I want the keys." He was doubtless mindful of the original price of the car, and he was probably not even going to ask for a postmaster's discount.

"You don't have enough money," Mellon replied.

If the owner of Scanlon Packard was paying $2000 for 1941 Clippers, albeit like-new examples, one can imagine what it took to get a new Packard in 1947. But that is conjecture.

Mellon drove the Clipper 46,000 miles, and when he sold it to Rick Reale in 1967, it was still in like-new, just-waxed condition.

"A lot of people were afraid of the Clipper when it came out," Miller recalled. "It was ahead of its years, with its aerodynamics. In fact, there's a lot about it that still looks modern, but it was too much future for a lot of people." Too much future: the very commodity Packard needed in 1941.

Final Years
1946-1958

THE DOOR DID NOT SLAM on Packard in Detroit; it creaked to a close in the autumn of 1956. No one day marked the end of the factory there. The workers did not rush out in tears, and the stockholders did not demand inquiries. Rather, the parent company, Curtis-Wright, started to save money by consolidating departments and shutting down rooms, and when they were through, there were no more costs to be cut, just gates to be locked.

"Not with a bang, but a whimper," as T.S. Eliot wrote, and in fact, without much of a whimper, Packard closed out 53 years in Detroit and 57 years as an independent automaker. What was left was shuffled into the Studebaker operation in South Bend, Indiana. Yet that ordinary day, when Packard left Detroit, hovers over every mention of the postwar Packard—unthinkable, but inevitable.

Because the crash did not come in a single day, there was time to save the Packard Motor Car Company. Throughout the years of steep decline, 1955-56, suitors were entertained and enticed, and the company's fortunes were discussed in the press. Morale at the plant remained high, considering the circumstances. All of the suitors walked away, though. The company had serious problems in finance, supply, and organization. Because of these problems, it is not a mystery that Packard went out of business.

The mystery is that it was actually allowed to go out of business. Packard had a name that had garnered respect before the war. After the war, it was perceived as an "old man's car," a tag that cursed it. Before the war, it had a place in the pattern of American life, but that very pattern was changed after the war. The establishment that Packard so neatly represented was part of a difficult past. The building of a bright new order was a juncture to let go of ikons like Packard and to find new ones. That is why Packard was allowed to fade the way that it did after 1956, into the past to which it belonged.

During 1955-56, as Packard's future ebbed, its parent-company, Curtis-Wright, acquired the franchise to market Mercedes-Benz cars in North America. Cadillac, of course, nabbed most of Packard's market share, but if any car can be said to have replaced Packard's blend of conservatism and engineering excellence, it would be Mercedes. With such opposite traditions, Mercedes was to become the new token of sobriety and luxury in automobiles—and Packard's owner knew it first.

In the postwar years, Packard tried to respond to the demand for new cars by adding a second assembly line in 1946. Space was so limited that the courtyard area between two main buildings was roofed in to make another great hall. Even so, shortages made production a nightmare, and the company had trouble lining up the most basic ingredient: steel. Three prewar suppliers had sold out and were controlled by other automakers. Still, Packard's purchasing department looked as far away as Austria and scraped together enough steel to endure.

Nineteen-forty-eight was the first postwar year to show excellent results, as sales rose to 98,897 (second-best in history) and profits bettered any showing since the Crash of '29. New engines and models were introduced in 1948, the engines being variations on that reliable bulwark, Packard's straight eight. Styling introduced in 1948 was generous and rounded and distinctive. As Alvan Macauley retired in 1948, the company observed production of the millionth Packard.

On the heels of the propitious showing in 1948, the Packard Motor Car Company celebrated its 50th anniversary in 1949. It was a prominent event in Detroit and altogether a high point from which the company's future seemed secure. The company had cash on hand and had developed a new gadget that competed head-on with General Motors: Ultramatic automatic transmission. In styling, the 1951 models snapped into a well-tailored look that removed some of the excess of the earlier models.

Packard looked down its nose when other automakers embarked on a battle for the highest horsepower in about 1953. Its straight-eight engine did not have remarkable horsepower, but it was smooth and capable of high speeds, if not thrilling acceleration. Packard waited for the public to come to its senses regarding horsepower, but that never happened. Packard's image suffered, despite youthful styling concepts such as the 1953 Caribbean. Doldrums set in as sales fell in 1954. Finally, Packard introduced a 225hp V-8 in 1955. By then, though, the slump had robbed the company of its cash reserves, and there was no money to advertise, no muscle with which to reverse the momentum.

In 1954, Packard had merged with Studebaker; the climate was just too raw in the Fifties for the independent automaker. Studebaker, however, had even deeper problems with finance than did Packard, and it was not a beneficial association. Curtis-Wright, a defense contractor, purchased Studebaker-Packard in 1955, not in the interest of saving Packard, however. After trying to sell Packard, Curtis-Wright closed it down and provided Studebaker with the name, to use on a handful of South Bend models in 1957 and 1958. Whatever the merits of these models, they were, in fact, products of Studebaker thinking, and so they are not featured in this book. In 1962, the "Packard Motor Car Company" was formally dissolved.

"Packard had really died in 1942," Ralph Stein wrote, voicing a common opinion. "It just didn't become official until 1962." In view of the glorious cars produced in the company's early and classic years, it is true that the final models were rather common, but Packard's inherent quality did not waiver. The company tried to make the transition to the all-out mass market, with at least a vestige of its old ways, and it tried to survive a business climate that vanquished every other independent automaker. One Packard customer of the Fifties bitterly blamed its demise on the postwar throw-away attitude: "Packard gave so much quality for the price that people didn't trust them."

The Packard Motor Car Company did not die in 1942, but for better or for worse, a settled view of the established order did.

"My grandfather was a Packard customer from 1906 until 1954," a man from Pennsylvania recalled in warm memories of the cars made by Packard. "In 1922, he bought my grandmother a Single Six phaeton. When guests came over in winter, she let them park in the garage and she left the Six outside. In the morning, theirs wouldn't start, more often than not, but hers fired on the first hit. We kept it until the Forties and called it 'Old Faithful.' "

"Every summer in the Depression," a Maine native said, "my family, which was large, had to visit our relatives in Iowa. One year, my parents bought a big, used Packard sedan and piled the whole family and a lot of luggage into it, so we could arrive at our relatives' feeling fresh. From then on, that Packard was only used on the trip to Iowa, but they never found a better car for the purpose."

"My momma was a maid for many years," a New York man said, "and she worked for a white family in California in a little town north of Los Angeles. They had a beautiful Duesenberg that she rode in many times. They also had a Packard convertible coupe, about a 1933 model, painted white. One summer, around 1935, Momma had to drive the Packard back to New York City for the family. She and my aunt and I went. It took us about a month. Lord, that was something!"

"When I was attending Smith College before my graduation in 1934," a New Yorker recalled of one of Packard's brighter moments, "I dated a student at Amherst who was quite an operator on his campus, selling enough bootleg liquor to buy himself a used Packard touring car. At Smith, there were dances that began in the afternoon, broke for dinner, and then continued until about eleven. I can see my date arriving for dances . . . driving up in his open Packard filled with Amherst boys in their tuxedos and top hats."

Remember Packard that way.

1947 Custom Super Clipper Seven-Passenger Sedan

A CHILD CAN USUALLY TELL at a glance what is important about a car, even a car 18 feet long, swathed in hushed elegance. Four children together can always tell. "We used to argue over who got to ride in the fold-out jump seats," recalled Nick Stoltz of the seven-passenger Packard purchased by his father, A.G. Stoltz, in 1947. "Or over who got to sit beside the back-seat radio. And we got scolded for running the antenna up and down too often."

A.G. Stoltz was a precise man, a banker like his father before him, at the Second National Bank of Bucyrus, Ohio. When World War II ended, he was still driving a 1938 Packard Twelve sedan, and he was ready for a new car. But Packard orders outstripped alotted steel, and Packard customers far outstripped cars in the showrooms.

One car that languished in a Packard showroom in upstate New York (where Stoltz relocated temporarily) was the Custom Super Clipper seven-passenger sedan. It was Packard's top-of-the-line car, the last one, indeed, in the traditional sense of Packards for the aristocracy.

The Custom Super Clipper chassis employed Packard's Custom Eight engine, with nine main bearings, producing 165 bhp. It was enough power to move the 4800-pound seven-passenger sedan to speeds boasted by performance cars of the day. Like a bear, it was deceptively fast.

"I remember a summer evening in the early Fifties," Nick Stoltz said. "Being in the car with Dad and a friend of his—

A.G. Stoltz and his new Packard in Bucyrus, Ohio, in 1947

the local police chief—when for whatever reason, they decided to find out how fast the Packard really would go. I vividly remember driving south out of Bucyrus on State Route 98, toward Marion, 16 miles away, after sundown. It was a long, straight stretch of road. Dad had his foot on the floor; I was in the back hunched over the front seat, and

there were six eyes glued on the speedometer as it edged past 100. At about 105 mph, he let up on it. I think everyone was satisfied and maybe a little uneasy."

But it was like floating on air, he recalled.

The Custom Super Clipper was a purposely steady car, balanced in all directions. The rear suspension benefited from a fifth shock absorber on the axle and a lateral stabilizer bar; in the front, an anti-roll bar reduced sway, and rubber insulation was used liberally to dampen vibration throughout. It is a heavy car to drive but not a clumsy one.

The design of the 1947 Custom Super Clipper was not remarkably different from the standard Clipper, except that it transferred the lines of that car, with its 120-inch wheelbase, to a 148-inch wheelbase, the longest in America that year. To make the seven-passenger sedan (and other Custom Super Clippers), Packard had no choice but to elongate and modify a standard Clipper body. The Briggs Body Company, contracted to produce all Packard passen-

Owned by R. Stuart Bewley

ger-car bodies, was pushed to the limit in 1946-47 and could not handle the deluxe models. Packard's commercial body company, Henney, produced the Custom Super Clippers by adapting standard Clipper bodies made by Briggs.

The handsome result, individually coachbuilt in the manner of prewar classic cars, was not suited to America's postwar mass market: Still, Packard's long wheelbase Custom Super Clipper accounted for total sales of 1772.

An era was closing, and A.G. Stoltz knew it. As a collector of antique cars, including a Pierce-Arrow and a Winton, he was sensitive to the enduring value of his Custom Super Clipper, and from the start, he saw it not as a family car but as a future collector's item: a future Winton.

"On the long, eight-hour trips between New York State and Ohio," his son Nick (the oldest of four children) recalled, "we were not allowed to eat, drink, or chew gum in the car. Sometimes we did chew gum and tried to hide it, but once, some of it got in the carpet, and that was the end of that." Wary of bubble gum, road salt, and hot rod drivers, Stoltz stopped using the Custom Super Clipper as his everyday car when it was less than a year old. Starting in 1948, he carefully stored it in the garage every winter.

In 13 years, Stoltz drove his Custom Super Clipper about 14,000 miles. In 1960, though, he was persuaded to sell it. To his family, it was "just a big, old car." It was big and old, but to A.G. Stoltz, not just a car.

1952 250 Mayfair Convertible

IF ONE LAST PACKARD DEALERSHIP is uncovered someday, by archeologists or men digging a new subway, and if it has a showroom filled with new 1952 Packard Mayfair convertibles, Murray Gammon could have them all sold by nightfall. He has been driving just such a model since 1952.

"Your cares are behind you in the Mayfair," Gammon would say to the prospective customer. "This car has never let me down. It starts very easily, and its full-leather seats are perfectly comfortable. There is a wonderful sense of security, aided by all of the tasteful appointments. I own several Cadillac convertibles of this vintage, and they do not compare at highway speeds and the top end. Simply put, they don't steer as well, ride as well, or drive as well as a Packard. And the quality engineering lent itself to minimal maintenance costs—it's cheap to run!"

Gammon is a hotelier in Victoria, British Columbia, and he owns The Classic Car Museum there: a hardworking man of means. What, the prospective customer might ask, does Mr. Gammon drive for a new car? Around town, he drives a company station wagon or the newest car he owns, a 1973 Cadillac. "If I'm going on a long trip," he said, "I'll take an old Packard; I don't really like new cars."

Gammon's father started driving Packards on business in 1915, and both his parents remained loyal to the name through the years, buying new models on a regular basis. After the war, the family came to appreciate their Packards more deeply, and they stopped trading them in. The six cars that collected in the family garages later formed the nucleus of the museum.

The Homestead Hotel in Banff, 1962: a snowy Mayfair is fourth in line

On Christmas morning of 1952, Enid Gammon, Murray's mother, couldn't help noting that her Christmas tree had sprouted a garland offshoot overnight, leading out of the living room, down the hall, and as she followed it, out to the garage. At the end, it was attached to the 1952 Packard 250, a gift from her husband.

That was just about the last time Mrs. Gammon got a good look at the car, though Murray seems to have loaned her the keys occasionally: He has estimated that she drove it 3000 miles and he added 85,000 more.

The Gammons bought the car from Packard Alberta in Calgary. The Mayfair bodystyle was soft and bright, like a kitchen fixture in the style of the day. The Mayfair convertible was the only open Packard sold in 1952. The 250 model, with an output of 150 hp, was at the middle of the Packard line. The previous year, the factory had begun installing Easamatic power brakes on the 250 chassis, which also had independent front suspension, an anti-roll bar, and lateral stabilizers in the back.

After World War II, the Gammons owned the Homestead Hotel in Banff, Alberta, a picturesque resort city that attracted a great deal of on-location movie production. When Murray Gammon was growing up, the Homestead Restaurant was popular with many celebrities, such as Robert Montgomery, Rita Hayworth, and Ali Kahn.

Owned by Murray MacLeod Gammon

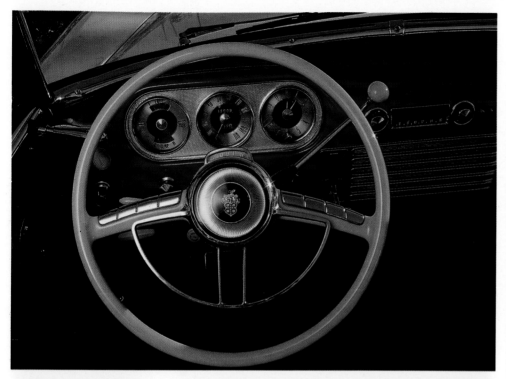

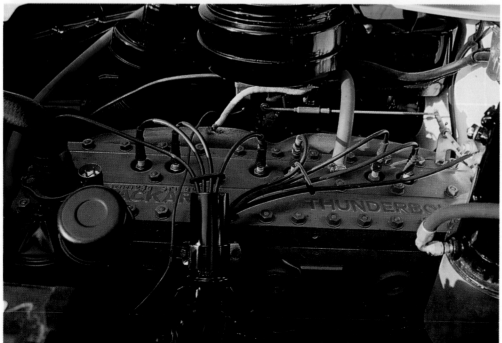

On the open road, the Gammons' Mayfair has topped 100 mph. "It isn't fast off the line," Gammon said. "But at 80 mph, it'll sail along all day. Other than sports cars, there weren't many cars that could keep up with it in 1952."

In the middle and late Fifties, Murray Gammon was in his teens, and he took the Mayfair everywhere around Banff and Victoria, where he attended college. On one occasion, when he was 18 years old, he drove it to the golf course but had to end the round when it got stuck in a sand trap.

Banff is better known for its winter sports, though. From January to April, it sparkles with clean snow and mountain air. When the sun was out and the wind was still, Gammon liked to drive the Mayfair with the top down through the mountains. Behind the quiet Packard motor, it was like a horseless sleigh.

One summer night in Banff, Gammon and his best friend went out to a dance and returned to the Homestead Hotel at around three in the morning. They didn't bother with the parking lot, but left the car on a lawn next door. At about three the next afternoon, Gammon happened to look out the window and noticed that the door was still open . . . and incidentally, the engine was still running.

"It wasn't even hot," Gammon recalled.

Sold.

1954 Patrician Sedan

T O EVOKE the automobile world of around 1948-54, when things were heating up in Detroit, it is enough to talk about transmissions. That is, to hear the optimism and guile in the names: ''Hydra-Matic,'' ''Power-glide,'' ''Dynaflow,'' ''Ultramatic,'' ''Fluid-Torque,'' ''Powerflite,'' and ''Merc-O-Matic.'' Packard played the parlor game as well as any of the others, calling its new brake system for 1951, ''Easamatic,'' itself an offshoot of ''Treadovac.''

The names could be a patter song by Cole Porter, but they expounded just as thoroughly as the public fancied upon automotive engineering principals. Likewise, a single, pocket-sized number denoting horsepower described engine performance to the satisfaction of most of the market. Packard's advertising copywriters could compete in the arena of jargon, but Packard engineers were by nature uncomfortable in the race for raw performance. ''There is a big difference between *horse*power and *driving* power,'' was Packard's response, prissy but true, to the horsepower frenzy. ''Driving power is 'usable' power and Packard gives you the greatest 'usable' power among American cars—at relatively low engine speeds.''

Sex appeal had crept, with a reckless jump, into the auto market, and ''usable power'' didn't have it. Even the 1954 Patrician, delivering 212 hp from a descendent of the same straight-eight engine that delivered 85 hp in 1924, seemed ho-hum. Cadillac cars developed 230 bhp that year—from a V-8. The market had learned about V-8 engines, that they

NO DEP 100714 — FORD MOTOR COMPANY — ENGINEERING STAFF — DATE 7-19-54

1954 PACKARD PATRICIAN (ULTRAMATIC TRANSMISSION) SIDE VIEW

FIGURE NO. 2

Prying eyes in Detroit: a photograph from the Ford file on Packard

had punch and verve and were very much the fashion.

Acceleration was a potent selling point in the mid-Fifties, a ritual that made every red light a significant opportunity. There was undoubtedly a reason why a victorious postwar society would place a premium on leaving thy neighbor in the dust, but the growing prevalence of sports cars may have

aggravated the matter. Among American cars, inherent differences were less pronounced than ever, as nearly all of them were competent and reliable. Evermore esoteric considerations—like acceleration from a standing start—gave cars identity and made certain models hot sellers.

The 1954 Packard line sold badly with its straight-eight engine and its usable power, despite ''Easamatic,'' ''Ultramatic,'' and ''Twin-Ultramatic,'' of which the latter was introduced late in the production year, to improve acceleration.

In San Antonio, Texas, in 1953, a black Packard Patrician was purchased by the Hosier family. It was the family's last Packard, or to be absolutely accurate, its second-last Packard automobile.

Mr. Hosier used the Patrician in his business, which was, as it happens, hosiery. The family vacation the following summer was to Kansas, and the Patrician was taken to Schmidt Packard in Wichita for service. The Schmidt mechanic had trouble with the car, or with a certain concrete

Owned by Robert McAtee

pillar in the service bay—but anyway, the two collided.

In the settlement that followed, the Hosiers moved themselves and their suitcases into a new blue Patrician, after the dealer installed air conditioning in it. Then they drove away. That was the Hosier's last Packard. The new car was full of options: a power antenna, four-way power seats, twin heaters, and foot hassocks for rear seat passengers.

Giving the family a whole new car was a typically magnanimous gesture on the part of the Packard company, though the unfortunate fact is that in the summer of 1954, it took such a disaster to dislodge a Packard from the showroom. Sales in 1953 had swelled to 81,000, but in 1954, they were down to 27,000.

The Patrician was the top of the Packard line, a distinguished and very comfortable sedan. The company promised a relaxed ride: The low engine speeds gave it a hush, while the power steering, automatic transmission, and power brakes were all of them the best in the industry.

The interior was swathed in a new nylon cloth, called Ma-

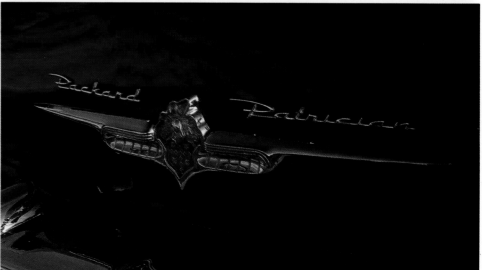

telasse, that looked bumpy but was actually smooth. The seats were designed to be orthopedically sound, with individually wrapped coil springs of variable tensility. All of the interior materials in the Hosier car are still those originally installed by Packard.

In 1955, Packard introduced its first V-8 engine, on models that sported an all-new look, and sales rose in response. In 1956, they slipped again for a variety of reasons. By then, the company was fading.

After one year with the Patrician, Mr. Hosier bought a Cadillac; Mrs. Hosier had the use of the Packard for the next 15 years. As a family, they took it on trips to Mexico and around Texas. In 1969, the Hosiers put the car up for sale. It had been decided that Mrs. Hosier was too old to drive; all the same, she was crestfallen to see the Packard go—either because she was watching her freedom depart or because the car itself had become an irreplaceable friend.

1956 Caribbean Hardtop

"I WAS GOING TO BE at Packard forever," Dick Teague said. "It was kind of naive, I suppose, but my father drove Packards for years, and like everybody else, I thought the company would be there forever."

Teague arrived at the Packard factory on East Grand Boulevard in August 1951, a designer under the aegis of Franklin Q. Hershey. He had worked at GM in the late Forties, and then he left for California to work in other areas of industrial design. When he was invited by Hershey to return to Detroit at Packard, it was a reawakening to the work that meant the most to him: car design.

Teague has been a car collector most of his life and owns three vintage Packards in addition to his 1956 Caribbean, a model that is part of his own history. "We produced some great show cars in those days: the Panther, the Request, and the Predictor. They had great youth appeal, as did the Caribbean among the production cars. The perception of Packard as an 'old-man's car' was contradicted by the work we were actually doing," he said.

"There were about 25 of us working in Styling," Teague said, "way in the back of the factory on Concord Avenue. Our morale was very high—Bill Schmidt [vice-president of Styling] kept it high by keeping us busy."

By 1955, all basic vehicle manufacturing had been moved out of the Packard factory. "We were alone at the back of this vast complex," Teague recalled, "and all the other lights were kept off. You could walk for hours through the empty spaces, just thinking about what it had once been. But back in Styling, we were busy tidying up the all-new 1957 models

Packard Styling Studio, 1955: Chief Stylist Dick Teague is third from right.

and even planning a facelift on the 1958 Packards." In January 1956, Curtis-Wright, which owned Packard, decided to shut down what was left of Packard-Detroit. After almost five years as chief stylist, Teague left in February 1956. "Even the day I walked out of the factory," he said, "and heard the great, heavy door shut behind me, I couldn't believe it

was over for the Packard company."

Teague went on to work at American Motors in 1959, where he was responsible for American, Javelin, and AMX models, as well as the bright, distinctive Pacer and Hornet models of the Sixties and Seventies. His last projects before retiring as vice president of design in 1987 were new Wagoneer models.

If he hadn't left Packard, if the company hadn't disappeared, if he had retired from Packard, as planned, just a year or so ago . . . "I guess it's easier to forecast what Packard would not have been," he said. "It would not have become overly influenced by the current jelly bean/sweet potato school of design dictated by the industry's near-preoccupation with aerodynamics.

"Packard would have produced a V-12 of the richest, most elegant, and prestigious appearance possible, coupled with a touch of nostalgia—no bells, whistles, geegaws, or kookie appurtenances—just a simple, well-proportioned, clean statement of noncontroversial design. Packard would have

Owned by Richard and Marian Teague

also incorporated several of the well-known symbols that gave all Packards great individual, exclusive road identity and 'car-isma.' ''

The foremost of symbols is the radiator grille-shape so famous in Packard's long and legendary history. ''The Nineties' Packard front would, however, be graced by a bright, recessed, and traditional central grille, vertically louvered,'' Teague mused. ''This jewel-like grille would be spring-loaded and surrounded by a soft-flexible, body color-keyed 'frame.' Other identity cues would also be incorporated, such as the red hubcap hex and cloisonne crests. The horizontal, ribbed side trim as used in 1955-56 would be updated as an additional identity feature. By the Nineties, this full wrap-around concept would be a most practical design element, containing all the exterior lighting units, as well as functioning as scuff molding. The aircraft-type upper structure,'' said Teague, ''would have a totally flush, glass-to-door relationship, and the doors would open into the center of the roof to make it easier to get in and out. The semiformal rear portion of the roof would be accented by a subtle bow break, as a small touch of past elegance.

''This vehicle would be powered by a twin-supercharged five-liter, V-12 engine,'' Teague continued, ''the third series Twin Six, in effect. This magnificent, Rolex-quality aluminum powerplant would propel the car to 65 mph in less than 10 seconds. The new, four-speed Ultramatic transmission would control a four-wheel-drive system, with antiskid, proportional disc brakes.''

Obviously, Dick Teague never really left Packard at all. He grew up knowing where the company had been, and he was carefully trained to know where it was headed in the future. His vision of that future appears at the end of this chapter: the 1999 Packard.

''It might have been,'' Teague said.

It is, though. It is.

The One-Hundredth Anniversary Packard

1999 Packard Twelve Patrician • Design by Dick Teague • Rendering by Ken Eberts